ADVENTURES IN THE LAND OF CANAAN

LECTOR HOUSE PUBLIC DOMAIN WORKS

This book is a result of an effort made by Lector House towards making a contribution to the preservation and repair of original classic literature. The original text is in the public domain in the United States of America, and possibly other countries depending upon their specific copyright laws.

In an attempt to preserve, improve and recreate the original content, certain conventional norms with regard to typographical mistakes, hyphenations, punctuations and/or other related subject matters, have been corrected upon our consideration. However, few such imperfections might not have been rectified as they were inherited and preserved from the original content to maintain the authenticity and construct, relevant to the work. We believe that this work holds historical, cultural and/or intellectual importance in the literary works community, therefore despite the oddities, we accounted the work for print as a part of our continuing effort towards preservation of literary work and our contribution towards the development of the society as a whole, driven by our beliefs.

We are grateful to our readers for putting their faith in us and accepting our imperfections with regard to preservation of the historical content. We shall strive hard to meet up to the expectations to improve further to provide an enriching reading experience.

Though, we conduct extensive research in ascertaining the status of copyright before redeveloping a version of the content, in rare cases, a classic work might be incorrectly marked as not-in-copyright. In such cases, if you are the copyright holder, then kindly contact us or write to us, and we shall get back to you with an immediate course of action.

HAPPY READING!

ADVENTURES IN THE LAND OF CANAAN

ROBERT LEE BERRY

ISBN: 978-93-5342-220-2

First Published: -

© LECTOR HOUSE LLP

LECTOR HOUSE LLP
E-MAIL: lectorpublishing@gmail.com

ADVENTURES IN THE LAND OF CANAAN

BY

ROBERT LEE BERRY

FOREWORD

This book comes out of our heart. It is intended to go to the hearts of others. Some of the things written here were learned by long and bitter experiences. Our "Adventures" were very real, and it is our hope that some of them our readers will never have. The real battles are fought within, and the struggle for mastery goes on in the soul, hidden in the mysterious depths of the spirit. Usually these battles are fought out alone, many times when others are not aware that anything of moment is happening.

Super-critical minds may not find this book interesting; we do not know; we wrote with no other intention than to bless the hearts and lives of the great common man and woman.

We hope you will enjoy this book. We hope it will do you good. If it does, our purpose will be achieved, and we shall thank God, whose help we gratefully acknowledge in the writing of this book.

R. L. Berry.

CONTENTS

Chapter   *Page*

INTRODUCTORY CHAPTER: THE LAND OF CANAAN. 1

I. GETTING READY TO ENTER CANAAN 3

II. THE CROSSING OF THE JORDAN 6

III. THE JORDAN MEMORIAL STONE 10

IV. TROUBLES OF LINGERING AT THE CROSSING 12

V. EXPLORING CANAAN BY FAITH 16

VI. THE BEST INHERITANCE IN CANAAN 21

VII. IN THE HANDS OF GIANT ACCUSER 24

VIII. CONFLICTS WITH GIANT MISTAKE 28

IX. IN THE DUNGEON OF GIANT DISCOURAGER. 33

X. THE TORMENTS OF GIANT BAD FEELINGS 38

XI. THE ROUTING OF GIANT DOUBT 45

XII. THE WINE OF PRAYER 52

XIII. PILGRIMS OF THE VICTORIOUS LIFE 55

ADVENTURES IN THE LAND OF CANAAN

INTRODUCTORY CHAPTER: THE LAND OF CANAAN

The story of the Israelites from their being in bondage in Egypt to their conquering Canaan is a type of the experiences of a man from his bondage in sin to his entire sanctification.

As a Scriptural basis for these remarks, see Galatians 3:6-29, where Paul, the great Apostle to the Gentiles, quotes a part of the Abrahamic covenant and applies it to Gentile Christians, the complete fulfillment of the covenant being expressed in verse 14, where the promise of the Spirit is spoken of as the "blessing of Abraham." It is also made plain in this chapter that salvation in Christ makes us "Abraham's seed," and therefore "heirs according to the promise." Hence the promise to Abraham has its complete fulfillment in New Testament salvation.

In Romans 4, Paul again dips deep into the promise of God to Abraham and brings forth beautiful teaching which shows that, to him, God's promise to Abraham was spiritual as well as material, that there was to be a spiritual seed as well as literal seed, and that "faith" is as potent as natural birth in making men children of Abraham. Also in these verses Abraham is made the "father of us all," even of Gentiles, which of course could not be true except in a spiritual sense.

The same subject is treated again in chapter 4 of Hebrews. Here the figure is "rest." The rest of the Israelites was their settling in Canaan, and in verse 6, speaking of the fact that some did not enter rest because of unbelief, allusion is made to the failure to enter Canaan from Kadesh-barnea. Then ten spies brought back such a bad report that the whole camp wept, and would not go over. For forty years these rebels wandered in the wilderness, until all were dead except Caleb and Joshua, the two faithful spies.

There is a beautiful analogy between the events of the Israelites in their journey out of Egypt into Canaan and the fundamental experiences of the Christian. Note these parallels—far too close not to have been planned as type and antitype by the great Author of salvation:

1. Abraham was promised two things: first, his seed should inherit the land of Canaan; second, in him should all families of the earth be blessed (Genesis 12:1-3).

2 ADVENTURES IN THE LAND OF CANAAN

2. Abraham was the father of both a literal and a spiritual seed, the first inherited literal Canaan and the second inherited spiritual Canaan (Romans 4; Galatians 4).

3. There was a rest promised both to the Israelite and to the Christian believer (Hebrews 4).

4. Israel was in bondage to Pharaoh and his taskmasters in Egypt, and sinners are in bondage to the devil and sin.

5. By a miraculous deliverance at the Red Sea, Israel escaped from Egyptian bondage; and sinners are saved by the miraculous new birth.

6. By another miracle of power, Israel entered Canaan through the bed of the Jordan River; and by a second work of grace, believers are wholly sanctified by the Spirit through the blood.

7. By refusing to believe and obey, the Israelites wandered for forty years in the wilderness, just as Christians fall away, grow lukewarm and backslidden many times when they see their privilege of being made pure in heart and refuse to walk in the light.

8. After the Israelites entered Canaan, they had to fight for their possessions; and so, too, do we have to fight for our spiritual possession in the state of holiness.

9. The literal land of Canaan was a good land, "flowing with milk and honey," where the Israelites ate the old corn and wine of the land. Just so spiritual Canaan is the best place of grace under heaven; indeed it is heaven's border-land, where saints have sweet communion with God and Christ and are ready for the great crowning-day.

In several chapters of this book we shall treat the subject of entire sanctification allegorically, using the types as prefiguring Christian experience. The battles of the soul against foes are real conflicts, which leave their scars and marks on many a Christian. Perhaps, out of the experiences of others, the reader will gather something of profit to himself, and be enabled to fight more effectively and not merely beat the air. There are spiritual powers in high places that challenge us to battle; blessed is he who has the armor, the courage, and the skill to win.

CHAPTER ONE

GETTING READY TO ENTER CANAAN

Can you tell me, please, the first step to take in obtaining the experience of entire sanctification? I have heard much about it, have heard many sermons on it, too; but the way to proceed is not yet plain to me, not so plain as I wish it were. Can't you tell me the first step, the second, third, and all the rest? My heart feels a hunger that seems unappeased, I have a longing that is unsatisfied; surely it is a deeper work I need! And so I plead, "Tell me the way."

* * * * *

Gladly will the endeavor be made to point out the way into the "holiest" of all (Hebrews 10:19). Probably the very first thing to know is that you must understand whether or not you are sanctified. Are you, or are you not? On which side of the Jordan are you, on the Canaan side or on the wilderness side? A definite answer to this question is essential. Sometimes there are doubts in your mind whether you are or are not sanctified. Well, let us first get rid of all doubts. The experiences of God in the soul are too definite to need their possession entertained with a doubt; and to know where we are spiritually is unquestionably our privilege.

If you find yourself on the wilderness side of Jordan, the next thing to find out is whether you are yet out of Egypt—whether you are justified before God, whether your sins are all washed away and you are a child of God.

If you are sure you are justified now, but have not by faith entered the Canaan experience—are not wholly sanctified—then you may know for certain that the experience awaits you.

Then there is one more very essential thing—you must believe with all your heart that sanctification is unquestionably an experience which the Bible holds out to all believers. Do you thus believe? If so, all is clear, and all you need to do is to go forward; or, in the words God used to Joshua, "Now therefore arise, go over this Jordan" (Joshua 1:2).

Do you need your faith strengthened in this particular doctrine? Let it then meditate and grow upon these promises and words of God:

"Wherefore Jesus also, that he might sanctify the people with his own blood, suffered without the gate" (Hebrews 13:12).

"Sanctify them through thy truth: thy word is truth" (John 17:17).

"And the very God of peace sanctify you wholly; and I pray God your whole

4 ADVENTURES IN THE LAND OF CANAAN

spirit and soul and body be preserved blameless unto the coming of our Lord Jesus Christ" (1 Thessalonians 5:23).

"Husbands, love your wives, even as Christ also loved the church, and gave himself for it; that he might sanctify and cleanse it with the washing of water by the word, that he might present it to himself a glorious church, not having spot, or wrinkle, or any such thing; but that it should be holy and without blemish" (Ephesians 5:25-27).

"Having therefore these promises, dearly beloved, let us cleanse ourselves from all filthiness of the flesh and spirit, perfecting holiness in the fear of God" (2 Corinthians 7:1).

After you have meditated on each of these texts for ten or fifteen minutes, consider these further promises concerning the giving of the Holy Ghost:

"And I will pray the Father, and he shall give you another Comforter, that he may abide with you forever; even the Spirit of truth; whom the world can not receive, because it seeth him not, neither knoweth him: but ye know him; for he dwelleth with you, and shall be in you" (John 14:16, 17).

"But the Comforter, which is the Holy Ghost, whom the Father will send in my name, he shall teach you all things, and bring all things to your remembrance, whatsoever I have said unto you" (John 14:26).

"That the blessing of Abraham might come on the Gentiles through Jesus Christ; that we might receive the promise of the Spirit through faith" (Galatians 3:14).

"And God, which knoweth the hearts, bare them witness, giving them the Holy Ghost, even as he did unto us; and put no difference between us and them, purifying their hearts by faith" (Acts 15:8, 9).

This great experience which Peter speaks of came to the disciples on Pentecost, when the Holy Ghost filled the whole company, and it changed a band of common men into the most powerful gospel band the world has ever seen.

Nothing feeds the soul as does the Word of the Lord. Meditate on the texts given, drink in the full meaning, comprehend what all of grace and love and spiritual power they hold for you; yea, consider at what a cost these blessings were purchased for you by the blood of the Lord Jesus Christ!

That you may see what your duty is in the matter, permit reference to these things:

On the cross of Calvary Jesus gave all, all for you and your salvation. There He cried, "It is finished." There He paid the last debt of all of us. There He proved His love, perfect, fadeless, unfathomable, boundless.

Go to the foot of that cross! See the Savior hanging there! Every motive that can move a soul finds its fountain there. Can you, in the shadow of the cross, be anything less than a full Bible Christian? Can you do less than give all to Him? Does not any selfish feeling or thought of holding back the full surrender seem sinful, utterly displeasing to your soul and to God?

GETTING READY TO ENTER CANAAN

Your duty, then, is clear. From henceforth you can not be less than all for Christ, you can not do less than go all the way for Him. Being a faithful Christian, you can not do less than your duty, once duty is clear.

Since conviction is a matter of knowledge, consider this: Christ's work hobbles along because there are so few whole-hearted, wholly consecrated souls to work for Him, whereas Jesus expects all to be whole-hearted in their service to Him.

Will you think also of the sin there is in the world, gnawing ugly wounds in the hearts and marring the lives of millions, and yet Jesus died to save every mother's child of them.

What is Jesus going to do if there are not a greater number of volunteers to carry on His work? For every sanctified soul is all the Lord's, ready for anything.

After Jesus died on the cross, He ascended to heaven. One day the angel Gabriel met Jesus and said: "Master, did you not suffer great pain on the cross?"

"Yes," answered Jesus simply and quietly.

"And, Master, that suffering was to redeem men to God, was it not?"

"Yes," answered Jesus.

"Well, how many know of your death and your suffering to redeem men? How will the world of sinners find it out? Have you made any plans?" asked Gabriel.

"I have told Peter and his brother Andrew, and James and John, and the rest of the twelve to go tell the people about it," said Jesus.

"Suppose they do not go?" asked Gabriel. "Have you made any other plans?"

"No, I am counting on them," said Jesus.

This is only a story, but it illustrates the point of how necessary it is for us to be consecrated and ready for the Master's service. Jesus is counting on us!

* * * * *

So you conclude you are still on the wilderness side of the Jordan? Very well, thank God you are out of the Egypt of sin, that the wilderness journey through justification is behind you, and that Canaan, that fair land where milk and honey flows, lies just before you. Only the Jordan intervenes. Of course the Jordan always is running strong and out of its banks every time, it seems, when souls are to cross, just as it was for Israel in Joshua's day. But this is only a necessary test to prove the sincerity and valor of the soul.

Thousands have made bold to strike their feet in Jordan's waters in the name of God and start across. You can see them over on the other side from where you are. Be encouraged; cross over the Jordan and enter the Canaan of soul-rest.

CHAPTER TWO

THE CROSSING OF THE JORDAN

Just how did you feel at the time you were sanctified? I have heard some tell of how the holy fire of the Spirit seemed to go all through them. Others have told of a deeper, more complete peace. Some have shouted for joy. Others have wept for joy. And I am wondering how one ought to feel. Can you tell me? And how can I know that I am consecrated? Every teacher of entire sanctification that I ever heard says that the consecration must be complete; but how am I to know when it is complete? I have consecrated over and over, but I do not feel certain that all, really all, is given up. Might there not be some self-will left that I do not know of? Please help me.

* * * * *

Probably it might not be wise to tell you just how I felt when the Lord sanctified me and made me whole, because it might tempt you to want the experience in the same way it came to me; and, besides, while the blessed experience is, in its essential features, the same in each case, yet each person has his own feelings and personal experiences along with it. These experiences are suited to each one's need; they follow the trend of one's natural disposition, and are a source of pleasure to us. The really important thing is to be wholly sanctified.

When Israel under Joshua arrived at the Jordan River, they were commanded by the Lord to "sanctify" themselves and prepare to cross over. This command to "sanctify yourselves" points to the perfect consecration that must be made before the sanctifying power falls upon us. Crossing the Jordan signified to them leaving the wilderness life forever behind them and entering upon a new life on the Canaan side. And in order properly to enter upon that new experience they were asked by God to set themselves apart by a solemn purification and consecration of themselves.

To begin with, then, let us consider what a consecration is, and next we shall consider the evidences of its being perfect and acceptable to God.

Several words and phrases cover what is meant by consecration, as "abandonment," "surrender," "lay all on the altar," "die," "subject the will to the will of God," "let Christ have his way."

"Abandonment" here expresses the idea that from now on your soul, your life, your interests, your time, talents—your all—are no more your own, but are abandoned to the will of God. You know how some people abandon themselves to

THE CROSSING OF THE JORDAN

a life of vice; they know no limit, but give themselves entirely over to it. Well, you are to abandon yourself to a life of holiness and service to God.

Did you ever see a potter at work on a piece of clay making a vessel of it? He gathers up a lump of clay and lays it on the wheel. As it turns and turns He builds up whatever it is that He wishes to make. The clay being inanimate, dead, yields absolutely to the potter, who makes of it whatever He pleases. This illustrates the abandonment you are to make— though with this difference: you have a will and reason, and your abandonment is to be the yielding of yourself to God because your clearest reason and most mature judgment tells you that such is best. From now on, instead of willing to do your own will, you are going to submit to God's will; for the most blessed thing in the world is the will of God.

Just here is where you may be tempted to draw back; for something may whisper, "Why, if you abandon yourself what will become of you? Maybe God would require of you something very hard for you to do. Is it not dangerous thus to yield?"

To illustrate this, suppose you are the mother or father of a boy. Like all boys, yours has given you more or less trouble by wanting his own way. There has been more or less of a battle of wills, his will against your will. You feel, and rightly, that your experience gives you a better idea of what is good for him than his experience gives. Suppose he were to come to you tomorrow and say: "From now on, Mother, I will do anything you want me to. I abandon my way and will for your way and will."

What would you do in that case? Would you make up your mind that now is a good time to put hardships upon him and make life as miserable as you can for him? "Indeed not," you would indignantly say.

Well, then, can the great God, who is love, take advantage of His children and, when they give all to Him, lay heavy and grievous burdens on them because He can? Just as you, when your boy yielded, would love him all the more and do all you could to make life pleasant even if there were some hard things in it, so God seeks to lighten the load His consecrated children must bear. To abandon yourself to God is an act of highest intelligence and wisdom.

"Surrender" implies the cessation of rebellion. Of course the sinner, to be converted, must surrender, and does surrender. And you have already surrendered in that way. Yet there is a self-life or a self-will that shrinks more or less from the will of God until we enter the Canaan of entire sanctification. This rebellion takes on the form of refusing or objecting to some of the Lord's ways with us. For instance, we may feel a call to special service—to the ministry, or to the missionary service, or to personal work—and we may have mapped out an entirely different life for ourselves and ate to submit to God's leadings.

Surrender of the will is a part of the consecration. There can be no inner soul-rest so long as our wills pull us one way and God's will pulls us another. When Jesus said His yoke is easy and His burden light He meant it is easy if we pull with Him, not against Him. How can two walk together except they be agreed? Then lay your will down; or, rather, actively, enthusiastically, delightedly will that

8 ADVENTURES IN THE LAND OF CANAAN

God's will be done in and with you.

"Lay all on the altar" is a favorite expression with many teachers of full salvation and the victorious life. The figure comes from the sacrifices made under Moses' law. Every Israelite had to offer sacrifices. The main thing about the sacrifice was, whether sheep, goat, lamb, dove, or something else, it had to be a perfect, unblemished sacrifice. God would not accept any lame, maimed, blemished, or otherwise marred sacrifice. It had to be the best of its kind. After it was brought to the priest and dedicated to the Lord, it was laid on the altar and consumed. It was the Lord's. The one offering it had no more to say about it whatever.

Then on God's altar you should lay all—time, talents, earthly goods, soul, body, and will. Once when Abraham had made a sacrifice, birds came to steal it. Abraham was careful to drive away the birds. A beautiful figure is found in Abraham's action. We might say that after you have laid all on God's altar you may need to guard the offering; for the birds of self-will, pride, unbelief, and evil desire may carry off your sacrifice.

"Die" is a favorite expression with other teachers of perfect holiness— die to self; die out to God; die to all but Jesus. The figure is full of vital meaning. Mrs. Cleaveland, in her delightful poem on the river of death, pictures the clergymen of various denominations as losing all their distinguishing marks as they cross the river, and over on the other shore not one can be told from another so far as sectarian peculiarities are concerned. This is even true of entire consecration, or crossing the Jordan into Canaan; for in Canaan there is a delightful absence of sectarian conflict; every one is too busy doing the will of God.

Dying is used to express consecration because some felt that the consecration was so acute that it seemed they had to suffer the pains of death. Others have not so felt. Whatever the feeling, there must be the dying.

Two women, one a widow and the other her daughter, lived together. They were both devout. The younger woman became sick, and grew worse and worse. At last all hope of life was gone, and mother and daughter began praying that the dying girl might have "dying grace."

The condition for obtaining this grace consisted in an absolute submission to die, a yielding of all to God's will; as she met the condition, so she received "dying grace." But the sequel was unexpected. While one receiving dying grace was supposed to die, this young woman lived and got well. But her "dying grace," as they termed it, was still hers. One day she spoke of it to her mother and said: "Mother, I am coming to believe that 'dying grace' is the grace we need to live by." And it is.

This young woman had made the deathbed consecration. God had accepted the sacrifice, had poured out His grace, and the young woman was sanctified wholly; and that was exactly what she needed to live by. She had died to self.

Now, how shall you know that all is given up and the sacrifice acceptable to God? This may well engage our attention.

First of all, remember that your will is your own, and that you yourself know what your intentions are. Whenever you decide to go to town to buy a hat or coat,

THE CROSSING OF THE JORDAN

you have no trouble in knowing your mind, do you? Of course not! And you can be just as sure of your mind or will in the matter of consecration to God.

You might begin this way: I desire to be wholly the Lord's: my will I desire to surrender; and my life I wish to be lived for God. Since the Lord in His Word has said, "By the mercies of God ... present your bodies a living sacrifice, holy, acceptable unto God, which is your reasonable service" (Romans 12:1), you may rest assured that God only awaits this surrender, and will be glad to accept it.

Now, do not only desire to be consecrated, but at once begin to count yourself the Lord's, permanently, irrevocably, for time, for eternity. Some, in the earnestness and intensity of their souls, in the solemn hour of their complete and definite surrender or consecration have written it out on paper, in the form of a will, and, signing it, have called on angels and God to witness the solemn act of their souls. But whether it is written out on paper or be simply the unchangeable determination within the heart, the point must be come to when all is yielded. There must be a final "yes" to God; the gift must be deposited on the altar, and from henceforth you are to consider yourself wholly the Lord's no matter how you feel about it. It must amount to a transaction, like the signing of a deed, or a contract, and when it has come to this point where you do actually hand yourself over to the Lord, body, soul, and all to be His forever, then you are to count the offering complete and the die cast forever.

Should you be tempted to investigate whether you "feel" that you are all consecrated, remember that your feelings have nothing to do with it. Your will is master here. As your will goes, you go.

> "When thy soul is on the altar laid,
> Guard it from each vain desire;
> When thy soul the perfect price hath paid,
> God will send the holy fire."

Do you lay all on the altar? "Whether is greater, the gift, or the altar that sanctifieth the gift?" (Matthew 23:19). If you have everything on the altar, your feet, like the priest's in Joshua's day, are dipping into the brim of the Jordan. You are ready to pass over. Just pass on over! Call the transaction closed. Your heart feels a deep security in handing all over to God, and there is the witness of your own soul that you have, now, given up all and God accepts the offering.

What next? Ask God to purge your soul until He is satisfied concerning its purity. Ask Him to kill all the things which displease Him, and destroy the last remains of inbred sin. Ask Him to restore the image of God in your soul, to come in and possess His temple. Ask God to fill you with the Holy Spirit, to let the Comforter take up His abode in you and abide with you forever. Swing wide open your heart's door to the Spirit. Believe that God does what He promised to do; believe He sanctifies you wholly. Since you are His, you are to trust Him to carry on this work in His own way. It is yours to yield and to believe. And we are "sanctified by faith" (Acts 26:18). Our hearts are purified by faith (Acts 15:8, 9). Let your faith wrap its arms around God's promise, and the work is done. Oh, marvelous grace of God!

CHAPTER THREE

THE JORDAN MEMORIAL STONE

One thing has always troubled me, and that is the witness of entire sanctification. How may one know all the time that He is sanctified? What is the witness to sanctification? Is it a feeling? an assurance? a peace? or what is it? Is it equally strong at all times, or does it come and go? If you can give me any information on this line, I shall greatly appreciate it.

* * * * *

One of the things that Joshua commanded the Israelites to do at the crossing of the Jordan has always been intensely interesting and suggestive. It was not a miracle, and there was nothing marvelous about it; it was just a thing that any man could do. When the crossing was being made, Joshua selected twelve men, one from each tribe, to do a special service. After all the people had passed over and the twelve priests were standing still in the River's bed, with the ark of God, Joshua commanded the twelve men to go to the middle of the Jordan and each take up a stone, place it on his shoulder, and carry it across to the camp in Canaan. Here the stones were to constitute a memorial: "And these stones shall be for a memorial unto the children of Israel forever" (Joshua 4:7). Joshua also set up twelve stones where the priests' feet had stood in the River; but it is these stones on the bank in Canaan that are of most interest to us.

We shall call these stones the "stones of testimony." They testified to a great fact, a great miracle, a great crossing, to the beginning of a new era in the lives of those hundreds of thousands of Israelites. Whenever an Israelite saw those stones, he was reminded of this fact.

Now, dear, seeking soul, as you cross the Jordan of entire consecration, the line between the place where you are not wholly consecrated and where you are wholly consecrated, the line between the time when you hope to be sanctified and the time when you shall know you are, as you cross this, carry out your stone of testimony. You have never passed this way before, and you need not pass it again; so get your stone of testimony now.

First note that this memorial was stone. It was not wood, that would rot, burn up, or float away to the Dead Sea. It was not gold or some precious metal that would be needed for other uses. It was not piece of parchment or paper upon which was written an account of the crossing. It was common, solid, enduring stone. So, too, the testimony of your sanctification is solid and enduring—as solid and enduring as the Word of God, the directions of which you have followed.

THE JORDAN MEMORIAL STONE 11

Notice also that this memorial was rather large, too large to carry around all the time, but was dropped and left as a reminder. There is of course an inner witness that is yours forever; but the crossing of the Jordan, that is, the obtaining of entire sanctification, is an event that will forever stand out as a time when you really received the experience of entire sanctification. There should be those witnessing spiritual realizations that differentiate it from all the other of your spiritual experiences. In short, it should mark your entrance into Canaan, the land of rest, of milk and honey.

What are these realizations? First, that you have been brought to a knowledge of God's will to sanctify you wholly. Next, you have definitely and solemnly dedicated yourself to God to be His and His alone forever. Then you have asked God to sanctify you according to His Word. You have believed that the work is done. All these steps are in direct harmony with what God said for you to do, and they, being carried out with the help of the Spirit, constitute the charter or receipt or evidence of your entire sanctification. You have met all conditions, and the grace is yours. You are sanctified wholly, filled with the Spirit, and you drop your memorial stone on the Canaan side of the Jordan.

As long as you remain true to your vows, to your covenant and consecration, you will continue in possession of your experience. You have no need of ever going back into the wilderness, much less to the Egypt of sin, but the fair land is before you—launch out and explore it. Enjoy for yourself the boundless riches of the grace of God and eat honey out of the rock.

CHAPTER FOUR
TROUBLES OF LINGERING AT THE CROSSING

Some time ago I consecrated to God for entire sanctification and thought I was sanctified. Then I began to doubting whether I was wholly sanctified; so I consecrated again. This I have done a number of times; in fact, so many times that I don't know what to do. Can you help me any in this difficulty? I am in doubts about my consecration. I am as consecrated as I know how to be, yet there is a feeling of unreality and uncertainty about it that is distressing, and I have found no way to end my distress. I am almost ashamed to tell how many times I have consecrated, and I am ashamed to tell the Lord that I am; for I have doubted so much that I am not sure of myself. My faith is weak also. If you can help me, I shall be very thankful.

* * * * *

The story of Pilgrim Exactly will probably be interesting, as well as helpful, to you. He told me the story. I will tell it to you as well as I can remember it.

Pilgrim Exactly crossed the Jordan for Canaan the first time twenty-two years ago, and he had never got away from the place where people cross over. Every now and then you could have seen him examining his memorial stone; and by and by he would pick it up, wade out as far as possible, drop his stone with a pathetic sigh, and then go on back to the wilderness side the best way he could. However, he did not stay over there long, but soon started for Canaan again. He always aimed to and vowed that he would select another memorial stone; but, mind you, he always came out with the same one he first brought over.

Do you ask why he did such a thing? The reason is simply this, brother: Pilgrim Exactly wanted to be so sure that he was in Canaan that he was never quite sure that he was there. He was not satisfied with the best of evidence. No one was brighter in the wholly-sanctified experience than he, nor did any one cross over into Canaan with any better evidence of his crossing than did he. But there is a bad, little, dwarfed giant named Doubtful, who lives close about the crossing-place, a half-brother to old Giant Doubt. Doubtful kept company with this pilgrim. More than likely that was one source of his trouble. The strongest pilgrims warned Exactly of the pernicious plots of this little, hard old dwarf, but he seemed not to heed their warnings.

Exactly would plant his memorial stone with a look that says, "It is done for the last time!" Then Doubtful would slip up to him, and this is practically what one present would have seen and heard:

TROUBLES OF LINGERING AT THE CROSSING   13

Pilgrim Exactly: "By the grace of God, I solemnly promise never to doubt my experience of sanctification again, no never. Lord, hear my vow, never, never to doubt again! I have staid by the crossing too long now. I must explore Canaan."

Giant Doubtful: "Good morning, dear Pilgrim. Are you sure you got this stone out of the right place this time? Seems to me, too, it is the same old stone you have brought over ever so often. You know you have never been satisfied with that memorial, and I do not see how you can be, either. Isn't it doubtful whether you really crossed the Jordan? Your consecration is likely faulty, and you know your faith is weak. Better be careful. You do not want to be deceived, do you?"

Exactly, wiping the sweat from his face: "That is a fact. This is the same old stone. My God, can't I get a better experience than this? O Lord, help!" And the poor Pilgrim would seem the very embodiment of distress.

Doubtful: "It is my opinion that something is wrong somewhere. Probably you crossed too soon. Maybe you have left something out of your consecration. By the way, were you not neglectful of duty yesterday? And then, you know, you promised God you never would doubt. Now just see, you are doubting somewhat at this minute. It is to be seen that you have failed somewhere. I believe you had better try it again. Something is wrong! you had better try it over." And dwarf Doubtful would rattle on much more in the same strain.

Just then Pilgrim Exactly would feel of his side, and his hand would touch the handle of the sword of the Spirit. Just when he would about draw it to deal Giant Doubtful a blow, Doubtful would say, "There can be no harm in being sure. If you cross over Jordan properly you will be satisfied, and it will not take long to go back and do a really thorough work of it."

At this Exactly wilted, dropped the sword, staggered toward his memorial stone, and, lifting it to his shoulders, limped back toward the Jordan to cross and recross again.

But the next day when Pilgrim Exactly got over into Canaan with the same stone, because there was no other stone in there when he crossed, as every man has his own stone, he would plant it as before.

One day, however, after planting the stone, he said, "By the grace of God, I am done with doubting."

When the little old dwarf Giant Doubtful came out that day, Pilgrim Exactly swung a terrific cut with the sword straight at the dwarf's neck. Doubtful never before ran so fast as he did getting away from that trusty sword. Since then Exactly has advanced into the land, overcome several other giants, and won a home for himself in Canaan.

The feeling of unreality which you have in regard to your consecration may be the result of your vacillation. No one can feel sure of his condition if he consecrates and then deserts his word, consecrates again and then doubts that. All of this should and must be cut off shortly by your honoring your own word and refusing to be confused about it. It can be ended by gathering yourself in hand in coming to a real, final conclusion in favor of your sanctification. If you are as

14   ADVENTURES IN THE LAND OF CANAAN

consecrated as you know how to consecrate, then that should be sufficient. In that case, all you lack is to bring the affair to a point, a conclusion, and give it all over to God, and let that be the end of it.

Now that you are ready to make this final decision, it will be worth while for you to examine your consecration. Are there any idols to which your affections fondly cling? Is it a delight to do something for Christ in behalf of others? Does it seem hard for you to give of your money to the blessed cause? Is prayer a burden? Are you really all the Lord's? Do not make the mistake of thinking a good disposition toward Jesus is consecration. To consecrate means to come definitely to the point of yielding all up to Christ once forever.

Possibly one reason for your feeling of unreality is because you can not see God and can not hear Him say, "I receive you." If God could be right before you as a visible person while you knelt and gave yourself to Him, you might think your experience more real. But it would not be. His word has been given, and it is "him that cometh to me I will in no wise cast out" (John 6:37), and He asks us to "bring … all the tithes into the storehouse, that there may be meat in mine house, and prove me now herewith, saith the Lord of hosts, if I will not open you the windows of heaven, and pour you out a blessing, that there shall not be room enough to receive it" (Malachi 3:10). Faith comes in all our dealings with God. He may appear not to notice us; but rest assured that He does.

Of course, after consecrating and doubting you have lost confidence in yourself; but this, too, should end quickly, and it will if you pursue a right course. To recover your self-reliance, self-balance, dismiss all the discouraging and doubtful thoughts about yourself. Take a real inventory of yourself. What are you, anyway? Are you honest? Does your word mean anything? Can you carry out a resolution? a decision? Very well then, refuse to be bothered about the past. Quit thinking of the past; utterly dismiss it from mind, and calmly and deliberately consecrate, and mean it.

Another difficulty in regard to consecration is that you may think you have lost yours when it is a trial sometimes to live up to it. You may think that to be consecrated means that every duty will seem delightful. In this you are mistaken. Did not Jesus, at one with the Father in will and mind, pray three times, 'O my Father, if it be possible, let this cup pass from me. Nevertheless not my will, but thine be done'? Some of the things God may lay on you or allow to be laid upon you are hard things, things which you will have to ask God for grace to do or bear. The crucial test, however, is will you do or bear them? If, in spite of the temptation to evade or go around God's will, you do obey, then your consecration is perfect.

Then, soul, end all this uncertainty, end all this unreality by coming now to the altar of God and placing thereon your whole self-life, body, soul, spirit, heart, talents, time, goods and gold, will, and all else. Tie it securely by one strong indomitable, irrevocable decision of your will. Count yourself all the Lord's. Begin to reckon and consider every event of your life in this light.

Allow nothing to come between you and God; let Him be first and be all to you.

TROUBLES OF LINGERING AT THE CROSSING   15

Please do not think of this dedication as in any wise meritorious, or capable of purchasing any blessing. It is nothing on these points. Consecration is placing yourself in an attitude or position where God can have His way with you. And this He asks you to do for your good. As long as any of your will stands in His way, He can not pour out the Holy Ghost upon you, and neither could you enjoy the fullness of salvation.

Nothing is quite so good as the will of God, nothing so adorable. In that will is bound up for you the noblest life, the fullest and freest expression of your individuality, the best adaptation and use of your talents, the greatest joy, the sweetest pleasures, the quietest rest, the purest delights in this world and pleasures forever at God's right hand.

Oh, embrace that will of God! Seek it, hide in it, revel in it, be enthusiastic about it, run to it. Oh, never evade it, fight shy of it, neglect it, nor refuse it! Dropping into God's will means dropping into our own niche in life and being happy in fulfilling our destiny as God has marked out by His infinite wisdom.

CHAPTER FIVE
EXPLORING CANAAN BY FAITH

I can not understand faith. What is faith, anyway? I try to believe; sometimes I feel that my faith is strong, but at other times I feel that my faith is giving way. Can you help me in this matter? Faith seems such a hazy, intangible, elusive thing; now I think I have it, now it seems certain I have it not. I feel at times that my faith is so strong I could believe anything, then again I feel that every bit of faith I had is gone. Can you give me any instructions that will help me?

* * * * *

Suppose we imagine we have an invitation to visit Caleb today (Numbers 13:30; Joshua 14:6-14), and we embrace the opportunity.

We should expect to find the old warrior at home on such a day because it is bright and fair; he did the most of his fighting in bad weather. It is not far to Hebron, where he makes his home. See, we are there now! Isn't the prospect from here beautiful and inspiring! To the north along the ridge is Bethlehem and Jerusalem; to the east the silvery waters of the Dead Sea glitter in the sun; westward is Gath, where Goliath the giant came from; and to the south is Beersheba.

Tell us, Caleb, some of your experiences in Canaan.

"Forty and five years ago I first saw Hebron. It was when Moses had sent twelve spies, of whom I was one, to determine the character of the people and land of Canaan. Long ago our father Abraham trod this soil, and God Almighty promised to give it to him and his seed for an everlasting inheritance. When I first heard of Canaan, down in Egypt, my faith was strong that it was a good land, flowing with milk and honey, as God said, and I longed to set foot upon it.

"When we twelve first left Kadesh-barnea for Canaan [Numbers 13:1-3, 17-33], I noticed that ten of the spies kept close together; but Joshua and I were eager to see all that we could of the land, and we ranged as far and wide as we could. Not far from where your feet rest now we got our first sight of the Anakims, giants of Canaan. They were giants indeed. Their legs looked like tree-trunks, and covering their faces was a dense growth of beard out of which their eyes gleamed like crystals in a haystack. The sight of them set my heart all aflutter, because I knew at once that they were very dangerous foes, not easily reckoned with. We were very cautious that they should not see us, and I must say that part of our company trembled violently with fear and, as soon as we got away a little distance, they ran with all their might.

EXPLORING CANAAN BY FAITH

17

"But something in my heart said that if God gave this land to Israel, then God would give us power over the Anakims, no matter how many or how strong they were.

"By and by we came to the walled cities. Joshua and I talked over the matter of taking them. While we could not see just how we were to do it, we decided that, since God had unmistakably promised the land to Abraham, and since He had already marvelously delivered us from the hand of Pharaoh, king of Egypt, and his dark bondage, and since He had helped us along through the wilderness and now had brought us to the very borders of the land, surely He expected us to have Canaan. And this I told to the others.

"'We can never take it,' they said, 'never in the world. Let us get out of here and back into Egypt as quickly as we can. We feel so faint. We can not conquer such a country. Why, see those giants, we are no bigger than grasshoppers by the side of them! And look at those walls, reaching almost to the sky! Let us get back.'

"'But if God said we should inherit this land, shall He not help us?' said Joshua and I.

"'We thought surely God promised us the land,' the ten replied. 'But we did not expect to have to fight for it. We supposed God would just give it to us without any fighting or trouble on our part.'

"'Oh, no, God never promised Canaan without a battle,' we replied. 'But He will help us fight, then we shall properly appreciate both God and Canaan and the fighting will make us stronger.'

"Well, we could not convince them, and our arguments fell upon very impervious minds, hardened as they were by unbelief and doubting [Numbers 14].

"Then for forty years we wandered in the black wilderness.

"Five years ago we crossed the Jordan, blessed be God. Those were great days in Canaan! God was very near us, and our foes trembled. Jericho fell down, Ai was taken, kings of darkness and giants of iniquity melted before the army of the Lord, until the land was in our possession.

"Then I went to Joshua and made known my request for Hebron, my home in Canaan. There were several giants making Hebron their home, and I was eager to dispossess them; for I liked the situation. Joshua gave me permission, and I marched toward it fully confident that our God would help me.

"There is no use to tell you the rest. Here am I, by God's help, at home in my possession. The giants are dead, and I hold peaceable possession by right of divine promise, the oath that God swore to our father Abraham that we being delivered out of the hand of our enemies might serve Him without fear in holiness and righteousness before Him all the days of our life [Luke 1:74, 75]. Thanks be to God for His great gift!"

We may visit Caleb again, since the recital of his conflicts and victories has uplifted our souls so greatly.

You say you can not understand faith. Let me ask you if you can understand

18 ADVENTURES IN THE LAND OF CANAAN

joy? or sorrow? or a heartache? or rapturous rejoicing? Can you find the cubic contents of anger? or measure love in bushels or weigh it on scales? And because these things are intangible and elusive, do you think they are not real? Indeed not! You love someone, and while you can not cube your love, nor weigh it, the reality of it you never question. So also with acts or decisions of your will. Who ever saw a will in action? And yet the outer life, in all its forms, is proof enough that a will has been functioning all the while.

Now faith is the same kind of thing as joy and love. It belongs to that family of intangible, unseen realities of life. They have to do with the spiritual part of our nature, and through them we rise higher or sink lower than we can through any mere physical feelings or actions. Faith, joy, love, are spiritual qualities, spiritual things, things of the soul, affecting it favorably or adversely according as they themselves are affected by causes good or bad. Doubt, unbelief, anger, wrong ambition, pride, and such are as intangible as are faith and love, but they are at the opposite pole.

Faith is no harder to understand than is doubt. Faith is believing, and doubt is not believing. One is the opposite of the other, just as heaven and hell are opposites. Considering doubters more closely, we find that doubters believe; but they believe the opposite of what they should believe. Doubters believe the wrong thing. A doubter is one who could and ought to believe facts, but for some reason or other can not bring himself to do it. Instead, he believes another set of things, which appear to be facts but are not.

Let us illustrate faith and doubt. You pick up a newspaper this morning and read that a fire destroyed a hotel in Chicago and four persons were burned, that a train ran off the track in Iowa and no one was hurt, and that a Congressman from Florida died. Do you doubt these facts or believe them! If you believe them, that is proof that you have faith. You look at the almanac and find it says that tomorrow there will be an eclipse. If you prepare to look at the sun through smoked glass, it is proof that you have faith. If you receive a letter stating that your uncle John died and feel sad at the thought of his leaving his family in destitute circumstances, it is proof that you have faith. If someone in your place of business brings you a report that fire has destroyed your warehouse and you feel at once the loss, it is proof that you have faith.

Then, of course, there are things which you doubt. You are told that some one has discovered perpetual motion. You smile, and do not believe it. You doubt. Doubt is simply the opposite of faith.

Now to show or illustrate how faith works instantaneously always, let us suppose you are a parent and one of your children is lost. It is your youngest child but one. You have hunted until you are exhausted, and find no trace of the child. Your heart is sick; a load as heavy as lead bears down upon you. You can think of a dozen different things that could have happened to the child; he may have been kidnapped, may have been run over and killed, may have fallen into the water and drowned, may be weeping his heart out somewhere. At last the whole neighborhood gets out to search, and you, exhausted, sit impatiently waiting. By and

EXPLORING CANAAN BY FAITH 19

by you hear some one halloo. Then you hear another. And then some one runs up excitedly and says, "The child is found, safe." The very moment you believe that news the load lifts, the heart is light, the soul is happy. Tears of joy flow freely.

But suppose it proves a premature report, and by and by another comes and says it is a mistake, that the child was found dead. Then all your joy is turned immediately to sadness. Faith always works instantaneously.

The quickness with which faith works has been illustrated by this: Suppose some one rushes into an office of philosophical, higher-critical professors, and cries, "Fire!" You would see those hard-boiled skeptics, if they believed the cry, rush unceremoniously and indecorously out of that building with all speed. People may scoff at faith working with lightning speed; but every exhibition of it only proves that it does.

Now you mentioned that at times you feel as though you believe strongly, and at other times you feel as though your faith is leaving you. You are making a great mistake mixing up your faith with your feelings. They never did mix; and all who try to mix them only get into trouble; for faith is one thing and feelings are another.

The only way for you to know that you have faith is to believe something. Do you believe anything? If so, then you have faith. Do you believe in God? Then you have faith in God. Faith is believing, just as seeing is seeing and hearing is hearing. If you see something, you know you have sight; if you hear something, you know you have your hearing; and if you believe, you have faith.

Faith in God is just like faith in anything else. God has said He will do or has done something for you. Do you believe He has done something for you? Do you believe He has done or will do that thing? If so, that is faith.

For instance, you have repented of all your sins and have asked God to forgive them. He has said that "if we confess our sins, he is faithful and just to forgive us our sins" (1 John 1:9). Do you believe this? You say, "Yes." Well, then, you have faith, and "by grace are ye saved through faith" (Ephesians 2:8), and, "therefore, being justified by faith, we have peace with God through our Lord Jesus Christ" (Romans 5:1). And, moreover, "he that believeth on the Son of God hath the witness in himself" (1 John 5:10); or, in other words, when you believe you know it, and God does for you what He promises to do.

The same reasoning holds good in entire sanctification. The conditions are consecration and faith. You are to put all on the altar, and ask and trust God to do the cleansing and give you the filling of the Spirit. Have you thus consecrated? Have you given all? If you say yes, then do you believe that God sanctifies you wholly? If you do, you have faith, and you are sanctified wholly, because God can not lie nor fail.

Faith in God, then, is believing God's Word, the Bible. Whenever you obey the Bible and meet the conditions laid down therein for any blessing promised, you may then believe that God does or is doing for you whatever He has there promised. And when you believe, you will have all joy and peace in believing, you will enjoy the riches of God's grace, and He will work in you mightily, as He does in

20   ADVENTURES IN THE LAND OF CANAAN

all those who believe (Ephesians 1:19).

CHAPTER SIX

THE BEST INHERITANCE IN CANAAN

I am troubled about my sanctification. My conversion was so bright and there was such a change that I never could doubt it. But when I was sanctified, there was not so great a change. And it was not so great as that of some I have heard testify. Neither do I feel as bold as some I have heard speak, neither did I taste such a death as others have testified too. In fact, when I compare my sanctification with what others say theirs is, mine suffers in the comparison. I have often repudiated my sanctification and endeavored to obtain an experience just like others'; but it seems I cannot. Must I try to obtain another, or be satisfied with the one I have? Any help you can give me will be greatly appreciated.

* * * * *

Suppose we go over to Bethlehem this morning; there is a Brother Faithful there whose acquaintance you positively will appreciate. He has been in Canaan a number of years and doubtless can tell us some interesting reminiscences of his life.

This is a famous place. Somewhere about here David killed a lion and a bear and composed some of those inimitable psalms of praise to God. In that field right over there Ruth gleaned for Boaz, and her maidenly purity won the hearts of all.

Here is Brother Faithful's house. Let us knock and go in.

"Brother Faithful, how did you happen to get such a beautiful home in Canaan!"

"Well, pilgrims, I did not just 'happen' to get it. The truth is, I did all possible to gain a home at Bethel, or on Moriah; either place seemed better than this; at least it did for some time, until I learned that here was where Jehovah wished me to settle. Bethel is close to where the tent of the Lord was pitched, and it has sacred memories of a ladder reaching up to heaven and holy angels ascending and descending on ministrations of mercy to man below. To me it, of all places, seemed nearest heaven; but, if I may reveal a secret, I have found that Bethel is not the only place that has associations of a ladder planted on it and reaching heaven.

"The reason I wanted to stop at Moriah was because I heard Brother Dreamgood who lives there tell of the remarkable experiences he had there. I began thinking there was no place in Canaan like that, and I did not stop to consider that all of us could not abide in one place. Brother Dreamgood told the wonderful story of angels and holy manifestations and heavenly illuminations constantly occur-

22   ADVENTURES IN THE LAND OF CANAAN

ring on that sacred spot till I forgot all about asking where the Lord would have me be, and forthwith started for Moriah. But I was baffled at every turn. Especially was I chagrined to find there was no place for me on Moriah at that time. Brother Dreamgood had a dreadful battle with the giants before he won a home for himself, and I am not certain that I could have fought them successfully.

"Then after that I fell in with Brother Worshipful who lived at Bethel. After he told of the good things there, I concluded Bethel was the place for me. But I made no headway in that direction.

"Having been in Canaan for some time and still unsettled, I began to inquire of Jehovah where He would have me be. It was made fully plain to me that God had the place for me that was best for me. A glad yielding to this truth brought great boldness to my soul. I girded on the armor, adjusted the shield of faith, grasped the sword of truth [Ephesians 6:10-17], and went where I was directed—toward Bethlehem, a place which I had regarded as palpably inferior. After severe fighting, I won. And I am satisfied."

* * * * *

Sanctification is a work wrought by God through the blood and Spirit. It is both a cleansing from sin and an infilling of righteousness. It has negative and positive aspects. It takes away from and adds to. Not that sin is a sort of root or germ. It is an evil that affects our nature. This evil is destroyed, and its effects banished. The Holy Spirit comes in, filling the nature of man with righteousness and purity. You must get your mind on the real work of sanctification, not on some of its special manifestations in some people's experiences. The manifestations of sanctification may be more specific for some people than others, because they may need such.

It is possible, too, that your conversion made a greater perceptible change in your soul and life than did your sanctification. This matter of change depends largely on circumstances. If you were very deeply convicted of sin and were very happily converted, your conversion may have been greater apparently than your sanctification. But these appearances are not essential considerations.

Still another point you must bear in mind, and that is that sanctification, while a separate and distinct thing of itself, is only the second step in a work already begun. Justification is essential to sanctification and is the beginning of those things that work full salvation.

During a camp-meeting one time a minister related a glowing experience he had when he was sanctified. He spoke particularly of boldness. He was made very bold.

When the altar-call was made, an old mother in Israel came to the altar. A minister asked her what she was seeking. She replied, with tears in her eyes, "I thought I was sanctified; but since Brother A— — testified to the boldness he received, I doubt whether I ever was sanctified. I did not feel that way."

The instructor carefully led her away from any comparison between her experience and others, and asked her if she were consecrated now.

THE BEST INHERITANCE IN CANAAN 23

"Oh, yes, just as consecrated as I know how to be!" she replied, weeping.

"Well, if you are all consecrated, what does the Lord do for those who are all given up?"

"He sanctifies them wholly," she had to say.

"And if you do not have as much boldness as Brother A — — said he has, probably you do not need as much. Or, if you really need more, would it not be better to ask God for more rather than to give up your experience of sanctification in a vain effort to feel as some one else feels?"

She saw the point, and her tears disappeared beneath happy smiles of joy.

There is yet another item you should consider. Many times those who testify so beautifully and graphically in describing their sanctification are under an inspiration, and the blessing is set forth in glowing colors. For the time being their trials and discouragements are forgotten, their struggles to keep the victory are out of mind, and they speak in the highest praise of the work God has done. In the exhilaration of the moment they magnify the work. We do not say they overdraw their experience; for really no tongue can tell it; but while they are all aflame with ardor and praise, you may be going through a trial. So, of course, their experience seems to outshine yours so far that yours suffers. But remember this—the time may come when you will be testifying as they now are, and they may be the ones going through a trial; then they may compare their experience with yours, and they may feel that they are the ones, who are behind. So compare no more. Be all for Jesus. If He gives some one seemingly a better experience, let Him have His way. What is that to you? Follow Jesus.

CHAPTER SEVEN

IN THE HANDS OF GIANT ACCUSER

I am having such dreadful battles! I have to fight, and fight, and there seems to be no end to it. Surely I am not sanctified; if I were, I should not be so tried. What shall I do? The desire to be all the Lord's is uppermost; but can I truly be all for Him with so many thoughts of all kinds running through my mind? Could I find rest from these battles probably I could feel that all is well; but with this constant battle I fear something is wrong. Isn't sanctification a grace where one will not be tried or tempted very much, at least not with such things as I am tried and tempted with? Why, the most terrible things ever heard of are suggested to me to do! Can you help me any?

* * * * *

Suppose we should visit a citizen of the land of Canaan and ask him if he had any battles with the giants of the land. No doubt the twinkle of his eye and the animated expression on his face would show that memory was at work, and we should wait in all expectation. Ah! here's one; let us hear him!

"Indeed, indeed. Many, many times did I battle with the giants of Canaan. Many people suppose Canaan is the home for soldiers to rest, while in truth it is the great battleground of the world. I recall one battle I had with Giant Accuser [Matthew 4:1-11].

"Look right over the top of that olive tree due east, down toward the Dead Sea. Do you see that shaded valley deep down between those two mountains? That is the Valley of Sorrows. In that valley I had one of the greatest battles of my life.

"It was before I possessed my home. I had been helping my brethren fight off the inhabitants of the land and was out at this time looking over the country. I entered that valley. The sun was sinking into the western sea, and my thoughts grew gloomy and foreboding. All at once right before me loomed the big form of one of the worst giants in all Canaan, Giant Accuser. I could not run back, the cliffs were too steep on either side to climb out, and the fierce old Giant blocked the way in front.

"'I rebuke you in the name of the Lord,' I said to him.

"'Ah, the Lord! Ha! ha! The Lord does not care for you. Steal that sheep you see yonder; no one will see you. If any one sees you with it, you can tell him a lie about it,' he said to me.

"I stood aghast at the suggestion. Never before had I had any evil suggestion

IN THE HANDS OF GIANT ACCUSER 25

like that, and I felt sick at heart that any such thought should enter my mind. The old Giant strode closer, and I trembled.

"'Curse and swear,' he roared at me, scowling down into my very face. And from his coarse mouth there rolled a volume of blasphemy such as I never had heard. The curses had a peculiar effect of sticking on my mind, until they seemed to be within me.

"I fell on my knees, while the old Giant dealt me a blow over the head with his club. 'You have cursed,' he shouted. 'See, your mind is full of evil words. And you would steal; for the suggestion lodged in your mind to steal that sheep. You are a sinner, that's what you are. Christians never have such thoughts as you are having.' And again he struck me with his club.

"I was too weak to fight. Finally I felt as if I really had sinned.

"The Old Giant then fell to beating me, and after half killing me and laughing right in my face and telling me he was going to drive me out of Canaan before he was through with me, he walked off.

"I lay there a long time thinking over the situation. Not an angel appeared, and God seemed to have forsaken me. My mind was all confused over the battle.

"While I was lying there, the old Giant came again. I was terribly frightened, because it seemed I had no weapon that he feared; if I had, I did not know how to use it. I tried to resist, and felt indignant within that he should treat me thus; but how to overcome him I did not know. I prayed, 'O God, help me! Help me!' But no voice answered, and no help came. The Giant strode right up and, without saying a word, again struck me with his club. The blow seemed to fall right on my heart, and a sickening feeling of utter discouragement and helplessness filled me. I groaned in complete confusion and bewilderment.

"'See how discouraged you are! You are not happy as are others in Canaan. Evidently something is wrong. People in Canaan ought not have such discouragements as you are having.'

"Then from some cause or other (it may be the Giant insinuated these things into my mind), a whole variety of slimy thoughts, vulgar words, bad imaginings surged through my mind and, together with a feeling that all was lost, seemed to dig down into the depths of my soul. There I lay, alone, forsaken, while the towering bulk of the Giant hovered over me ready to club me back into utter helplessness any minute. Finally I attempted to rise; but down came that dreadful club. Once more I struggled to my knees, determined to arise; but a terrific blow just at my heart felled me again.

"'You have sinned,' he hissed. 'You can not stay in Canaan. God has cast you off. See, He has abandoned you. He loves you no more. Die and be done with it. You are a sinner, anyway; you might as well do something desperate and end all.'

"I was so confused, I hardly knew what to do. The Giant dealt me one more blow, then left me to nurse my wounds.

"Finding myself alone, I began to endeavor to collect my thoughts and find the

ADVENTURES IN THE LAND OF CANAAN

significance of the encounter. But my mind was so confused that the more I tried to reason out the why of the affair, the more confused I became.

"And then, to my consternation, the Giant came in sight again. I knew instinctively that he would once more beat and wound me. I made a feeble attempt at resistance; but it seemed to avail nothing. He repeated the beating I had before, and there I lay utterly baffled. The same thing occurred for many days.

"Then one day my attention was called to the shield of faith [Ephesians 6:16] with which the Lord had equipped me. I had used it slightly, and there it lay at my feet. And my sword of truth lay unused by my side. Why I had not used it was a mystery to me. No giant can stand before it. I then and there determined that if Giant Accuser came again to beat me, I should use these holy weapons.

"Not long after this decision was made, the Giant came again. He came up confidently, expecting to make short work of me and laugh at my calamity. I did not shout at him, nor utter any sigh of despair as before, neither was I trembling; for I now knew that all I had to do was to use my weapons. When the Giant got close enough, he bawled out again, 'You have sinned. Your thoughts have been on things that are wrong. You have doubted. You must begin over. You are lost.'

"'You are wrong,' I declared. 'I am a full citizen of Canaan, with a clear title to a home in this land of Beulah,' and with that I kept before me my shield of faith, and drew the sword [Ephesians 6:17] and struck at him with all my might. He winced, but immediately again braced himself. He was not sure but that I might yield; so he began telling me the wrongs and sins he was accusing me of.

"'I am not a rebel,' I declared emphatically, 'and these ugly things coming to my mind are from you, old Giant Accuser,' I added. Then I struck at him again with all my might. He gave way a little at that, and I saw it, and it gave me immense encouragement. Then I rained blows on him as fast and hard as I possibly could. Soon he started to run. Summoning all the strength I had, I ran after him, giving him blow upon blow, until he jumped into a deep place and disappeared. Then I dropped on my knees and praised the Lord God Almighty for helping me win so signal a victory.

"I have fought with Giant Tempter, Giant Discourager, Giant Covetousness, Giant Liar, Giant Lust, Giant Pride, Giant Doubt, Giant Fear, Giant Worldliness, and many others. Thank our God for the weapons of warfare, the shield and the sword, the breastplate and the girdle, which give us power over them. I have not seen a giant for some time; but if any of them should attempt an encounter, by God's help I am ready."

* * * * *

Sanctification does not deliver from temptations; but it does make us more sure of winning over them. It is even probable that you will have more battles to fight, have more temptations to overcome, after you are sanctified than before. The spiritual foes are by no means confined to the justified state; there are a host of them to meet in the Canaan experience.

Many newly sanctified people have been overwhelmed, just as you have, with

IN THE HANDS OF GIANT ACCUSER

dreadful inner battles. Either the mind is harassed with constantly recurring evil thoughts, or evil words keep popping into it till they apparently spring from within. Or perhaps the suggestion to commit some sinful act keeps persistently coming to mind. Maybe feelings one considers foreign to the sanctified experience possess one. Possibly some diabolical temptation keeps whirling one about. All of these are sent with the avowed object of overthrowing the soul.

It is a favorite method of Satan's to suggest a sin or bring something bad to the mind and then accuse you of being guilty of the evil. It is as if a thief should turn around suddenly and accuse the owner of the stolen property of being the thief. Satan may fill your mind with bad things and then try to throw the blame for having them all on you. His object is so to trouble you that you will give up your faith, after which he will make short work of you.

Fight on! No one can grow strong without fighting. And the battles give proficiency in the use of the spiritual weapons. When your faith is assailed, you learn how to use the shield of faith. Then in the next assault you can use it more familiarly. The same reasoning applies to the using of the sword of the Spirit, which is the word of God. These very battles which seem to be more than you can bear are only developing that which will make you a strong and valiant soldier in God's army.

Then, too, these violent spiritual battles are proof of your ability to resist, else you would not have them (1 Corinthians 10:13). They are proof of your trueness. So, instead of looking upon them as something to be frightened or troubled over, see in them a signal proof of your strength and of God's confidence in you. So, then, dear soul, be encouraged concerning them; rejoice that God counts you able to fight for Him and counts you able to win. By looking at them in this light you will make of them a source of encouragement. That being the case, let the battles come—they will do you good (2 Timothy 2:3; 1 Peter 1:7).

CHAPTER EIGHT
CONFLICTS WITH GIANT MISTAKE

I make so many mistakes, it seems I am just a bundle of contradictions. I try to do good; but at times my efforts are so crude that I seem to do more harm than good. What shall I do? And though all the time I try hard not to make mistakes, yet I still make them. It seems to me that surely I am not sanctified, or else I should be more perfect. Do not the Scriptures command us to be perfect even as our Father in heaven is perfect? I am not perfect; far from it. Really I must be very imperfect. Is it right for me to claim to be sanctified? Can you help me?

* * * * *

Let us visit some of the pioneers of Canaan today and ask them to tell us some of their experiences. Let us see if Faithful is at home. He has a possession in one of the most charming vales of Beulah, and the beautiful flowers blooming there and the luscious fruit growing there tend to make him one of the happiest citizens of the country. I am just certain that he will be glad to tell us a story.

Here we are close to his home now. Oh, see the garden! Just like the Garden of the Lord.

See, it is just a little longer than it is wide, and is fenced with a row of protecting flowers called Grace. The central feature of the garden is that beautiful white lily called Love. It looks as though unusual care has been bestowed on this plant; see how it towers above the rest so grandly and yet is so majestically humble. Its fragrance spreads far and wide. Doesn't it make you want to sit down under its magnificent foliage and drink in of its glorious essence? Over there on the left of Love is a group of flowers of different species. That large cream-colored flower is called Patience. That crimson one is called Joy, and that with broad, drooping white petals is Humility. The sweet perfume you notice in any part of the garden is from Humility. That pink blossom on the right is Peace, and a very pleasant odor it has. Next to it is Faith. See it? It is a remarkably robust plant. Notice its blossom of pure gold color. It has no perceptible odor. This flower here, with all the colors mixed most intricately and beautifully together, is called Goodness. No wonder Faithful is so happy and cheerful, with such a garden! [Galatians 5:22, 23].

Oh, hush! There is Faithful on his knees now, at prayer to the Almighty!

How sublime he looks! Come; he rises.

"Good morning Faithful."

"Good morning to you, pilgrims. Blessings upon you in the name of Imman-

CONFLICTS WITH GIANT MISTAKE   29

uel.

What may I do for you?"

"We are pilgrims in Canaan and have only lately crossed the Jordan. We seek a home. But we have heard of the giants and we saw one afar off, too. We are a little afraid. We thought probably you would tell us how to overcome these giants. Will you!"

"With the greatest of pleasure. One of my greatest joys is to teach pilgrims the strategy of spiritual warfare and tell them how to overcome the Anakims of Canaan [2 Corinthians 10:4].

"About the first giant I met in Canaan was one Mistake, a large, loose-jointed fellow, who, I found, made a tremendous bluster but was as weak as a pygmy. Really he is not a true Anakim, but a Gibeonite, who are foes until they are conquered, and then they become hewers of wood and drawers of water for us—they become our servants betimes [Joshua 9:21]. But at first Mistake assumes all the characteristics of a true giant.

"Not long after I crossed the Jordan, I met him. He came lumbering down upon me, and I thought my days in Canaan were numbered. It was only after I made some blunder or said some tactless thing that Mistake bothered me, but at such times he gave me untold trouble. One time a pilgrim named Slow was standing by the way. As I was passing him, I, not being as careful as I should be, bumped into him and nearly knocked him off the road. Poor fellow, he began to cry, and said he was ruined and believed that if such was the way pilgrims treated each other, he would go back into Egypt. This, of course, caused me to feel very sorry. I went back and apologized the best I could, but it hardly consoled him. I started on. And, do you know, up came Giant Mistake! He caught hold of me and gave me a sound thrashing for what I had done [1 Peter 2:20].

"But really, Mistake did not cause me so much trouble as did Giant Discourager. This Giant Discourager is a true giant, of pure Anakim blood, and he is in the habit of accompanying Mistake. And so it was that every time I met Mistake, old Giant Discourager was with him. Giant Discourager beat me unmercifully nearly every time I met Mistake. He would flog me within an inch of my life and throw me down so bruised and bleeding that I almost wished I was dead [1 Kings 19:9-18]. It was only when I made a blunder that Mistake and Discourager beat me; but as I made these nearly every day, my life grew very miserable. I was about to conclude that Canaan-land had lost all its milk and honey; for I had not found very much of either yet.

"It got so that I anticipated the approach of these giants, and they never disappointed my anticipations. Giant Discourager would call me all kinds of names, such as a sinner, a perfect failure, a no-good, a weakling, a coward. And he would tell me, 'You have no faith,' 'You never will get a home in Canaan,' 'You will be cast out at last,' and many such like things would he say to me.

"When in my very worst battle with Mistake and Discourager, old Giant Despair came around to see me [1 Kings 19:4]. He claimed that by my repeated fail-

30   ADVENTURES IN THE LAND OF CANAAN

ures he had the right to possession of my soul, and he said he was going to carry me to his dungeon and club me to death, just as he almost did Bunyan's pilgrim, Christian. This frightened me nearly to death.

"In the very extremity of this bitter battle, an angel of Immanuel, named Solicitude, came to my side one day and said, 'I will teach you how to tame Giant Mistake and how to put Giant Discourager to flight.'

"'Oh, do tell me!' I cried.

"'Well, here is your shield of faith. Take it and hold it up. Quit dragging it around in the dust behind you. Here is your sword of the Spirit, get it in your right hand and use it. That is what it is for. It is not for a mere ornament, nor a mere appendage, as you have made it. Use it. Pull the girdle of truth up a notch or two, tie your gospel shoes on tighter. Press the helmet of salvation upon your brow. And when the giants come, fight [Ephesians 6:10-17; 2 Corinthians 6:3-10, 7:5-7].

"'And, really, so far as Giant Mistake is concerned,' the angel Solicitude went on to say, 'he is not a true giant. There is no Anakim blood in him. He is a Gibeonite; all you need to do to him is to conquer him, and he will be your servant. You can never get entirely rid of him even in Canaan; but by tactful management he can be of some service to you [Hebrews 12:5-11]. But Giant Discourager—you must win over him; for he has slain many a poor pilgrim, and waits to slay you.'

"I thanked Immanuel for sending Solicitude to tell me the secret of warfare and how to handle Mistake and Discourager. And it was even so. I made my blunders as usual, and Mistake and Discourager came falling down upon me. I ignored Mistake. But I gripped my sword, held up the shield, and made for Discourager, giving him a terrible blow over the head. He challenged me there, and broke forth at me in awful epithets; but I let the sword fall as fast as I could wield it. Pretty soon he ran in a disgraceful riot of retreat and plunged down a dark canyon which they say is his home. When I looked around, Mistake had shrunk up to about half his former size.

"'You come with me,' I said to him, 'I can't get along without you; but you must behave yourself from now on.'

"'I will,' he said. And he always has since."

The story of Faithful makes us feel better, doesn't it?

Sanctification purifies the motives, and makes the spring of impulse and action pure; but it does not give maturity of judgment nor perfection of reason. If an ignorant person is sanctified, he will find keenness of perception as regards right and wrong, but he will still be ignorant.

Sanctification does not imply that a sanctified person shall not need to study and advance in knowledge (2 Peter 1:5-9). Though sanctified we are still human beings, and we must utilize the common means to knowledge just as others do. Sanctification affects the heart, and its work is to take out evil, the sin in the nature, and make it holy and pure. Also it means an infilling of God's Spirit, which pervades our nature after sanctification just as sin pervaded it before. But sanctification does not eliminate humanity from our nature.

CONFLICTS WITH GIANT MISTAKE 31

Mistakes, therefore, are the common lot of all—sinners, believers, and sanctified ones.

Not only are we liable to mistakes, we are inseparable from them in our earthly existence. As one grows in experience, knowledge, and maturity of judgment, one's mistakes may become fewer in number; but no one on earth can ever expect to get entirely beyond making them.

Let us take a look at some illustrations: A young Christian had a father who drank. One day another Christian saw this Christian young man go into a saloon. He reported it around that he saw this brother go into a saloon. Well, the young brother must have backslidden, was the instant conclusion, and so it was reported. But the young man had gone into the saloon to get his father to go home. A very noble act; but the story that was told was very detrimental to the young man. It was a mistake to tell that he was backslidden without first knowing the facts of the case.

A mother has three children. One of them comes running in crying almost as hard as it can, and says, "John hit me with a stick." Mother calls John and punishes him for hitting Sister with his stick. By and by Mother finds that John did not do it, but that a playmate did. A mistake was made.

Sometimes one hears something detrimental to the character of another. On the strength of this, one may pursue a certain course of action. By and by it may be found that this first report is not entirely true to facts, and one regrets the course of action taken. A mistake has been made.

Mistakes are made in every department of life, mental, spiritual, physical; in the home, in school, in the laboratory; in mechanics, in business, and in government. It is simply impossible to know always what to do or to say. Mistakes, more or less, are occurring all the time. Many of the things we know we have learned by our mistakes. A farmer becomes successful by eliminating the mistakes of the past, by ceasing to do the things that proved to be inefficient. A manufacturer becomes successful by eliminating the weaknesses of his product, by eliminating his mistakes. So with every department of life.

Maturity is gained only by experience covering a period of time, hence sanctified people will have to learn by their mistakes just as others do, and by observing closely they are able to eliminate many mistakes and live more happy lives.

Our Father knows our limitations, and he will not cast us off for our mistakes. Do not count mistakes as sins. For some of your mistakes you may ask pardon, of both God and men; but do not allow discouragement to come in. Be happy along with your mistakes.

There is a strange but natural law of the mind that works in this way: If you make a mistake and worry and brood over it and live in the fear that you will make a similar mistake again, you are liable to make the same mistake—over and over, as often as you fear making it. Someway or other the agitation over it invites it to return. There is a certain attraction your fear and agitation creates toward it, which, even though you abhor it, draws you in it again and again. On the other

ADVENTURES IN THE LAND OF CANAAN

hand, if one makes a mistake, and, after promptly asking forgiveness, if necessary, promptly forgets it and goes on as if nothing unusual whatever had occurred, he will find that he will hardly make that mistake again.

Here is a secret for the newly sanctified ones; you will make mistakes, but learn to confess them fully and broadly and completely, and, after doing that, then to refuse to think any more whatever about them. Let God take care of you and also of the mistake.

Imperfection of human disposition and character is a fruitful source from which mistakes arise. Here is a person so slow as to be a trial to nearly every one about him, while here is another who, because he is so fast, is continually injuring the feelings of others. Here is a person naturally so impatient that at times he wounds and hurts others. The intentions of these persons are often misunderstood, and mistakes arise from the misunderstanding. We, thinking that certain things were done or said for certain purposes, may do and say certain things. Later we discover some other course would have been wiser and better.

So, dear anxious soul, do not expect to get beyond making mistakes. Profit by those you make. Use them as stepping-stones to a better experience. Keep consecrated, keep your faith clear, and commit yourself to God, mistakes and all. Sanctification makes us pure; but it takes time and experience to make us mature.

CHAPTER NINE

IN THE DUNGEON OF GIANT DISCOURAGER

I feel very discouraged at times, and sometimes the spells of discouragement hang on for a long while. I wonder if I am sanctified. From unaccountable sources, bad feelings of every description depress my soul, and along with these bad feelings come doubts that cast gloom over me. I have prayed and prayed that these feelings of discouragement might leave me; but they have not done so. I despair of prayer bringing me the help I need. Really, I know not what to do. I earnestly desire to be all the Lord's and have His will done in my life, and it is painful to believe that these discouragements hinder God's will in my heart. How do sanctified people feel, anyway? I should think they ought to feel ecstatic joy all the time, being so consecrated and near the Lord as they are. I need help on this line, and will appreciate any advice you give me.

* * * * *

The Wilderness of Canaan is a wild, rough district bordering on the Jordan Valley, through which every pilgrim and home-seeker must pass before he finds his home site and settles down. Some pilgrims are fortunate in passing through it quickly, while others, coming under the spell of two old giants who live there, have a very hard time passing through. These giants are Discourager and Despair, said to be twin brothers, sons of a bad mighty couple, Unbelief and Doubt, who live in the same wilderness and are, they say, the grandfather and grandmother of one of the worst families of giants in all Canaan. It is in this Wilderness that pilgrims encounter Giant Accuser, a cousin of Giants Discourager and Despair.

It is said that Pilgrim Victory had a long and hard battle with these two giants, Discourager and Despair. We shall have time this evening, so why not visit Victory? Probably he will tell us of this battle. We should like to know how he overcame them. We hear these two giants are really afraid of him since he has become so proficient in the use of the sword.

Very well, let us visit Pilgrim Victory.

Where does he live? He lives on Mount Moriah, and we shall find him at home, no doubt.

Oh see, here is a monument by the roadside! Let us stop and read the inscription. Oh! Listen!

"It was on this spot that a desperate battle was fought between Pilgrim Victory and two of the worst giants in Canaan, Giants Discourager and Despair. Victory

34 ADVENTURES IN THE LAND OF CANAAN

won after a long fight. The castle of Giant Despair is situated in one of the dark ravines to the right. In clear weather it can be seen from this spot. Pilgrims are warned to be prepared to meet these giants, for they have slain their thousands."

Come! Let us hurry away from this place! But look! See! There is the castle of Giant Despair! It looks more like a jail, or prison, than a castle. Maybe there is some poor pilgrim in there now. O Immanuel, if there is, send an angel to tell him to use the key of Promise so he may get out!

Why, here comes a pilgrim from that direction now. And there comes old Giant Despair after him. O Immanuel, help!

Will the pilgrim escape? The old Giant is coming so fast! But it is clear today. Yes! now the sun bursts full on the old Giant! Ah! he seems to melt in his tracks. Oh, yes! now we know why—he can not run in clear weather. Here is the pilgrim on the main road again.

"Pilgrim, we are so happy to see you get away. You look so worn, so weary. And there, what can that be, poor fellow? There is blood and wounds all over your back. That is where the old giant beat you, isn't it? How did you escape?"

"Blessed be Immanuel forever! For a long time old Despair has had me in his dungeon. I've been nearly killed. Giant Discourager encountered me first and got me off into that ravine over there toward the castle. Then old Despair caught me and put me in his dungeon. He beat me regularly morning, noon, and night. He has killed a number of pilgrims. He killed one while I was there; and there is a large heap of the bones of other poor pilgrims out of whom he drove the spark of hope. But this morning I thought of a key called Promise [1 Kings 8:56] that Bunyan's pilgrim told of, and to my surprise it fitted every lock I had to open. The old Giant ran after me. I do not know what happened to him; I did not look back to see. But I am safe, anyway."

"Come on with us, we are going to visit Pilgrim Victory. What is your name!"

"My name is Honest."

"Well, here we are on Moriah. And yonder is Pilgrim Victory! He seems to be polishing or sharpening his sword. Why, it shines like silver now!"

"Blessings on you, pilgrims, and what can I do for you?"

"Oh, Pilgrim Victory, tell us of your battle with Giants Discourager and Despair, will you!"

"To the glory of Immanuel, yes. And I shall begin with an early experience, and this is the way it came about: No sooner had I crossed the Jordan than Giant Mistake began to keep me company. Not long after that, Giant Discourager joined us, much to my detriment. I should have fought him then; but he said he had a right to travel with pilgrims, and I did not know any better; so I let him stay in my company. When we got farther into the Wilderness of Canaan, Giant Discourager began to torment me awfully. Every day he beat me, till I had no strength left. I did nothing but sit and nurse my wounds for many days. According to Giant Discourager, I was a failure; and it did appear that way. I was not good for anything, he

IN THE DUNGEON OF GIANT DISCOURAGER   35

said, and there was much truth, apparently, in that saying, too. He said Immanuel did not care the least bit for me; and it did look that way. 'You will never get out of this wilderness. You will never be able to do any good. You will always feel miserable,' said Giant Discourager to me. In fact, he saw nothing ahead for me but woe, failure, misery, and despair. And it appeared certain that he was right.

"Just at that place where you saw the monument, I fought the battle through, and won. But I was in Giant Despair's dungeon two weeks at that. It was after I escaped that I fought the fight I won. I had got out of the dungeon by using the key of Promise; but the weather was foul, and the giants caught me at that spot.

"The battle was a long one. With all the subtlety of his lengthy career, Giant Discourager threw out every idea and insinuation to get me to give up. But while these insidious attacks were very hard to ward off, I had definitely promised Immanuel down in the dungeon that if he would get me out I would never be caught in company with Giant Discourager again. I saw while there that it was my keeping company with him that got me into Despair's hands. So I had to keep my promise.

"But Discourager would not leave; so I swung at him with my sword, and said, 'Get thee hence, Discourager, I am Immanuel's. I am a citizen of Canaan, I am across the Jordan, this is my home; here my rest shall be. Get thee hence' [Luke 4:1-13]. His foul breath blew over me, and his awful concoctions of unbelief and despair almost overthrew me. At that, Giant Despair grabbed me, and was in the act of lifting me bodily and carrying me away, when a fierce desire to fight to victory possessed me. I made another stroke at Giant Discourager and then aimed one at Despair. This freed me. Then, gathering myself, I rushed at one, then the other, until I chased them back into their haunts. Oh, victory, how sweet! And how blessed it was after that not to have that old Discourager's heartless and despairing conversation poisoning my thoughts! Oh, what a relief!

"On thinking of it, I then and there purposed to build the monument you saw on your way here. Many a pilgrim has taken warning and escaped an awful death.

"Pilgrim Honest, I know those are tears of gratitude flowing down your poor face; but dry them, and come with me. I will bathe those wounds of yours and give you food that will relieve all your distress [Isaiah 66:10-13; Matthew 12:38-21]. And to you, pilgrims, we say farewell."

"Good-by, Pilgrims Victory and Honest. May it be well with you."

Now let us talk between ourselves.

It is no sin to feel discouraged. The only place where sin can enter in connection with discouragement is in entirely surrendering faith and letting actual transgressions follow. When the soul is tormented to the point where it appears impossible for it to claim the victory any farther, that is no evidence that that soul has sinned and is lost. In this case God sees the soul as it really is; He does not look at the soul's own estimate of itself. Many a sanctified soul has given up faith for sanctification, and even for justification, merely on the strength of some argument the devil has presented. For instance, a person may consecrate all, have perfect

36 ADVENTURES IN THE LAND OF CANAAN

faith, and receive the experience of entire sanctification. In a week or two this person may make a mistake, or for some reason or other he may begin to have bad feelings in himself. Satan now sends his tempter to accuse the soul and cause it to doubt its having the experience of entire sanctification. After a painful struggle, the soul feels, that, on the evidence presented, it must give up its profession of a sanctified state, and does so. But God, looking down, sees that that soul is just as consecrated as ever, and loves God as much as ever. He can not hold that soul as it holds itself. So while the soul despairs, God holds it as all right. The only reason the soul does not get God's view is because these doubts and accusations obscure God's will and promise, and the devil's doubts are admitted instead of God's word.

That more souls are done to death by discouragement than by any other one thing is probably a true saying.

You say you are discouraged. Over what? Is it because you do not have the pleasant feelings you would like to have? This is no cause for discouragement. You may be better than you feel, just as many are not so good as they feel they are. Feelings are no standard to go by. Is it because you can not accomplish more? Do the best you can and be satisfied with that. Is it because you make many blunders and mistakes? Care not for it, for all make them. Profit by them and go on.

Discouragement is deadly to the soul. It is a destroyer of hope, faith, confidence, joy, service, and victory. Look at the discouraged man! There he sits. Nothing seems good to him; and he hesitates to do anything. What army ever won a victory if it was discouraged? What merchant ever succeeded in business when discouraged? Who ever accomplished anything when discouraged?

Vow never to give way to discouragement. Sign the pledge against indulgence in it. Why not? Discouragement is the effect of the devil's work. Will you engage in helping the devil at his work?

There is no sound argument in favor of becoming discouraged; there is no reason or logic on its side. If you have obstacles to overcome, discouragement will make them only that much harder to overcome. Do you make mistakes? Discouragement will only make it harder to overcome them. No matter what may be your trouble, or failure, or other problem, discouragement is a positive hindrance. And if it is given way to, it must ultimately be overcome, in addition to overcoming the obstacle which occasions the discouragement, before one has the victory.

There is one thing you will do well always to remember, and that is God's promise in John 3:16. No matter where you are, no matter how hopeless everything seems, no matter how far down you may get, even into sin— remember that God loves you and has this promise, exactly suited to your need. All you have to do to begin to get out is to step upon that promise.

Yes, sanctified people feel discouraged at times. But since they are all the Lord's they must not give way to it, but must pray and trust Him to carry them through. This sooner or later brings them through the trial (1 Peter 5:10). Jesus Christ never gets discouraged. Let us be like Him in the eternal hope of the triumph of the grace of God (Romans 8:37-39). In which triumph we may have a share both while we

IN THE DUNGEON OF GIANT DISCOURAGER 37

live here and again in the heaven of heavens.

CHAPTER TEN

THE TORMENTS OF GIANT BAD FEELINGS

I am just a bundle of feelings. I never imagined one could have such a variety of them as I am now experiencing. Most of them are bad ones and I am greatly disturbed by them. Really, I doubt whether I am sanctified, on account of the feelings I have. Do sanctified people always feel joyful? I have heard that they do, and if it is true that they do, then I am not sanctified. Big doubts take up company with me every morning, and so long as I feel as I do I do not see how to dismiss them. My heart is heavy, very heavy, over these questions. Can you tell me how sanctified people feel? Please do, I am so anxious to know.

* * * * *

Nearly every pilgrim in Canaan has met Giant Bad Feelings, a doughty old giant with a long bad record for troubling pilgrims. He is not, they say, so dangerous to life as are some of the other giants, as he rarely slays a pilgrim; but for inflicting torment on them and as a helper to Giant Discourager no one can equal him. He is a most pestiferous giant, with a numerous family.

This is going to be a fair day, the sun came up clear this morning; shall we visit Pilgrim Sunshine? She lives in one of the sunniest, most pleasant vales in all Canaan, so I hear. You think it will be profitable to go over to her home? Very well, let us go.

By the way, did you ever hear the story of Pilgrim Sunshine? It is said she used to be sad, broken-hearted, fearful, and despondent, and that she lived long in the Valley of Sighs. Of course, we want to hear the story from her own lips. She has had a great deal of trouble, has pilgrim Sunshine; enough to make one despair, almost. Her people persecuted her, her husband deserted her, her sons reproached her; but, nevertheless, she is one of the happiest inhabitants of Canaan.

I believe we are nearing her home now, see how clear the air is up here, and the flora is getting more bountiful and beautiful, isn't it! There is her place! What a lovely garden she has! And it is growing out of such rocky soil! There she is, the dear old mother in Israel! When we get to her, note the marks of care that line her saintly face; but notice also the sweet smile that graces her kind countenance. Oh, that we could bear up under life's cares and burdens as she does!

"The Lord's blessings be yours, Pilgrim Sunshine."

"Aye, and the riches of His great goodness attend you, pilgrims. Sit down under this amaranthine bower and rest yourselves."

THE TORMENTS OF GIANT BAD FEELINGS   39

"We are new pilgrims in Canaan and we want to settle somewhere in the land. Some one said the Vale of Hidden Delights is a good place to live in. Seems to us it is. Could we find a home here? And we should be glad to hear you tell us some of your adventures in Canaan. Coming along, we saw some giants. Do any giants live in this vicinity? We are hoping that we can gain our inheritance without meeting any of them. Can we?"

"Pilgrims, I could wish you might settle into your inheritance without a battle; but I have never yet heard of a case where a pilgrim did so. It is true some more sturdy and valiant pilgrims have little trouble with the giants and soon win, but many have hard battles to fight [Luke 12:28; 1 John 5:4]. As to your settling here in the Valley of Hidden Delights, remember that it is only by the greatest toil and care we are able to bring loveliness and beauty out of this rocky soil. But if Immanuel allots you a home here, do not fear; some of the sweetest fruits and flowers of Canaan grow right here.

"My hardest battle was with Giant Bad Feelings. Beware of him! I had a pensive soul, a sensitive nature, and was conscientious to a scruple [Romans 14:1-6]. Bad Feelings took advantage of this fact and caused me trouble untold.

"I was very happy when I crossed the Jordan into Canaan, and set up my memorial stone with a shout. I advanced into the land to explore it at once. The old corn and wine of Canaan delighted me [Joshua 5:11, 12]. My weapons of warfare were bright, and I felt able to meet any foe. But inadvertently I got into the Valley of Sighs, and lived there far too long. I blame Giant Bad Feelings for it, yet I should not have allowed myself to be influenced by him.

"It was not long after I had passed Jericho that Giant Bad Feelings accosted me.

"'Good morning, pilgrim,' he said, 'how do you feel this morning. Seems to me your feelings are not what they should be. Pilgrims in Canaan ought to be happy all the time. You are not happy. There is a little load on your soul. See, you are carrying burdens!' and at that he laid something heavy upon my shoulders. 'It is true,' he chattered on, 'that pilgrims should be always happy, and you are not. That is plain to be seen. Now, be honest about it, aren't you sad?'

"Well, I had to confess I felt bad.

"'Certainly you feel bad. Are you sure you are all consecrated to Immanuel? Are you certain you left all the love of Egypt behind, on the farther side of the Jordan? Something must be wrong with you since you feel as you do.'

"At that he blew something into my face that sickened me with feelings of discouragement and dejection. Really, I felt worse than I did before ever I crossed the Jordan. I felt faint and sad.

"'Probably you have failed somewhere! More than likely Immanuel has cast you off, and some giant will carry you out of the land. You are a failure. That is all there is to it.' And with this he struck me a hard blow that seemed to land right on my heart. I fainted and fell.

"After this, Giant Bad Feelings visited me every day. He had the power, it

40 ADVENTURES IN THE LAND OF CANAAN

seemed, to make me feel just as he desired. At times he would throw over me feelings that imitated envy, anger, and such like. When Bad Feelings would shroud me with ingratitude to Immanuel, then he would turn around and beat me for the ingratitude just as though the feelings were my own. And really it was here that Giant Bad Feelings deceived me. He had manufactured these feelings himself and, on encountering me, would lay them upon me, all the while insinuating that they were my very own. He would bring bad words to my mind, bad thoughts, ugly pictures and ideas that my soul and mind revolted against. He would deftly cause it all to seem as though it came from my heart. And then he would lay the most miserable and heart-deadening feelings upon me possible.

"Finally some pilgrims found out that Giant Bad Feelings was causing me much trouble and they visited me. 'Pilgrim,' they said, 'pay no attention to Giant Bad Feelings. He is a big blusterer, anyway. Ignore him. Next time he comes tell him plainly that you belong to Immanuel, and that your feelings are consecrated to Jehovah. Tell him that if Immanuel allows you to have feelings you do not understand, that is Immanuel's business, and must be a blessing to you in some way or other.'

"Giant Bad Feelings came around as usual after this visit of the pilgrims.

"'Good morning, Pilgrim Sunshine. Not much sunshine in your soul today, is there?' he bawled out.

"'Perhaps not,' I said. 'But I belong to Immanuel, and the state of my soul is in His keeping.'

"'Oh, pshaw! you feel miserable, and you know it. Be honest! And be sure! you might be deceived if you do not investigate very closely the state of your feelings. Remember, as a man feels so he is, according to Beelzebub.'

"'I am Immanuel's,' I declared vehemently. 'How I feel is His concern. Whatever the feeling He allows, there must be good for me in the experience. Anyway, I am His and He is mine.'

"'Come now,' said the Giant. 'Do you mean to say that you believe you are all right when you feel as you do! Be careful!'

"'Yes, sir, I mean to say that very thing. I believe I am all right, no matter how I feel. You have been lying to me. Get thee hence' [Matthew 4:1-11; 1 John 5:4, 2:12-14].

"At this I swung at Bad Feelings with the trusty sword of the Spirit. It was a hard struggle, but at last I chased him away. Then I moved out of the Vale of Sighs to this Vale of Hidden Delights."

"Oh, we feel so animated over this recital of your battle and victory over old Giant Bad Feelings, Pilgrim Sunshine! If he attacks us we believe we shall know what to do. Our armor and weapons are proof against him, this one thing we know. Oh, Immanuel, help us use the weapons thou hast so graciously put in our hands!

"Farewell Pilgrim Sunshine."

THE TORMENTS OF GIANT BAD FEELINGS

Now let us do some considering. Probably seventy-five per cent of the people who consecrate all to God for the grace to live the victorious life are troubled over the state of their feelings. It is so natural to think that if one wholly abandons all to Christ, that one thereafter should at all times feel joyful, close to Jesus, be conscious of His presence, feel the love and peace the Christian has. In general, *feel* at all times that all is well. And when one's feelings are opposite from this, a serious question and doubt usually arises as to whether the soul is really in Canaan-land or not. The fact is, one's feelings are no standard to go by; for they are subject to a variety of conditions, spiritual, mental, and physical, and change and fluctuate in a very swift and unaccountable manner many times. The ups and downs of the Christian life would indeed be violent and serious if they followed our feelings; but our faith tells the real story, not our feelings (Ephesians 2:8, 3:17; Romans 8:28, 37-39).

When you are tempted to regard your feelings, ignore the matter altogether. Look in another place for evidence of your standing. How is your consecration? (Romans 12:1-3). How is your faith? (1 John 5:4, 10). Are you all the Lord's? Do you still believe His promise? If you can say yes to these questions, you are still on victory's side, though you may not feel it.

The will, not the feelings, is the controlling factor in life. The feelings are like a family of children who may, if allowed to grow up disobedient and unruly, cause one much trouble, but if controlled and made obedient, contribute to one's happiness. Feelings are a part of us. Christian experiences are felt; that is, they affect the emotions as well as the will. Feelings fluctuate, and, in fact, in many cases become very unruly, like spoiled children, and want everything their own way. Bad news will produce sad feelings. If you receive a letter today announcing the wedding of a friend, you rejoice; if it announces a death, you sorrow. If you are sick in body your feelings may partake of the quality of your physical condition. It is well that our feelings enter into our lives in this way, else we should lack the sympathy, love, and other emotions that are essential to social happiness. So let us thank God we have feelings; they connect us with the joys and sorrows of others. But let us not gage our Christian experience by the way we feel.

Sanctified people have feelings that are natural. Man was created with all the social instincts before the fall. Before sin came in, he was told to multiply and replenish the earth. Out of the two natures, male and female, arise all the social instincts that produce families, homes, laws, and governments.

Man, however, is twofold in being, with soul and body in union. Soul and body function together and each affects the other. By steadily thinking you are sick, you can become sick; by overexerting the body, the mind can be deranged; etc.

Sanctification restores man morally to where he was in Eden. Sanctification cleanses away the nature of sin and leaves all the God-given instincts intact.

Without trying to be technical, we may set down man's natural instincts and feelings as follows:

Man's nature as created by God had capacity for love, joy, sorrow, justice, fear.

ADVENTURES IN THE LAND OF CANAAN

These may be called basic instincts. There are phases of these we may profitably mention and discuss in connection with how or what a sanctified person may feel.

A sanctified person may feel: (1) The working of the law of self- preservation. (2) Sorrow at the death of loved ones. (3) Pleased when receiving words of appreciation. (4) Rising of righteous indignation at times. (5) Impatience at the slowness of justice or the wrong actions of others. (6) Pleasure in social life. (7) Craving of sex impulses and desires. (8) Hurt when illy spoken of or to. (9) Heavy through many temptations.

Taking these in order, let us explain them more fully. And we shall give here the results of over twenty years experience in the sanctified life, and many of these facts have been learned by bitter experience.

1. Self-preservation is a natural law. Fear is a part of it. Perfect love casts out fear, the fear that is slavish and results from sin; but perfect love does not destroy all timidity nor the sense of the need of protecting one's life. A sanctified person has just as good a right to run to a storm-cellar when a cyclone comes as has any one else. One form of fear is timidity. A newly sanctified person may feel somewhat timid in performing some duty. If, however, God's will calls to duties that mean even death, the fully consecrated soul goes on. So in such cases the law of self-preservation gives way to the higher law of self-sacrifice for Christ's sake.

2. Sorrow at the death of loved ones is compatible with sanctification. Many other things cause sorrow, such as disaster, disease, and sin, and these affect the wholly sanctified. The sanctified, however, have the Comforter to help support them and assuage their griefs.

3. If a sanctified person receives words of appreciation, he feels pleasure; not that they exalt him, but that they create in him a natural joy at being so appreciated. It is said by some that sanctified persons are "dead," and the point is illustrated by saying that pins might be thrust into a dead man and he will not wince. If sanctification destroyed the natural feelings, it would be a disaster rather than a blessing. It purifies them, but does not destroy them.

4. God planted in man the sense of justice. God made man in His own image. What we find in God, we find in man. God is just; so the principle of justice abides in man. Sanctification destroys the selfish vindictiveness of anger, but it does not destroy the sense of justice, and a sanctified person will feel the rise of a righteous indignation at evil. This is illustrated in Jesus, when He "looked round about on them with anger" (Mark 3:5), and also when He made the whip of cords and drove the robbers out of the temple (Matthew 21:12, 13). If the righteous man can not feel indignant at evil, how can God judge the world? Justice implies anger at evil. If righteous anger is wrong in man, it is wrong in God. Because God is God does not mean that He can do a moral wrong and it be right because God did it. His acts must be intrinsically right of themselves. Therefore, on the fact that He will judge the world we predicate the righteousness of sanctified indignation. And this is not carnal anger, which raves and slays and destroys unmercifully and wickedly.

5. It is rather hard to divide impatience into a just impatience and an unjust impatience. The point may be too fine for definition, but Scripture and experi-

THE TORMENTS OF GIANT BAD FEELINGS   43

ence both prove that sanctification does not make one perfectly patient. In fact, who should judge as to what perfect patience is if it were a possible attainment? Sanctification does make us patient. The constant ruffling of soul over untoward events stops. We grow patient. We trust God. We wait and hope. But we read that "tribulation worketh patience" (Romans 5:3); so hard experiences make us patient, that is, if we bear them. James says, "The trying of your faith worketh patience" (James 1:3). So what tribulations and trials work is not completely done by the Spirit when we are sanctified.

6. It used to be said by some that sanctification destroyed social instincts to the point of making social diversions distasteful. It seems very hard to disentangle the true state of holiness from asceticism. Once, holy men were supposed to be dead to social enjoyments—they would not marry, they would not wear ordinary clothing, they would not associate on a common plane with their fellows. But Jesus did not live that way. He made wine for a marriage feast; He ate dinner at a rich Pharisee's house; He enjoyed being at Martha's home. John leaned on His bosom at the last supper. Jesus was no ascetic.

Sanctification lifts social contact to its highest level. Brilliant conversation on a plane of purity is as enjoyable to holy people as to others. Figures of speech, puns, and riddles may mark the conversation of holy people as well as others. Yet their talk does not descend to the vulgar, frivolous, giddy, jay chatter of the wicked. As is said of conversation, so may be said of parties and picnics, which are names for outings or gatherings of various kinds at which refreshments may or may not be served. Should God's children be debarred from these pleasurable associations because the world goes too far in them?

7. Sanctification does not destroy sex impulses, but it does ennoble them and bring them under control. Hence the drawing of natures to each other is common to all, and courtship and marriage are honorable, as Paul said.

8. Since sanctified persons can appropriately feel pleasure at words of appreciation, so can they feel hurt at slights and impositions heaped on them by others. Perhaps the dividing line between what is right and what is wrong in this matter is this: so long as one feels hurt but does not feel like hurting in return, he may be safe; but when one is hurt and then feels the retaliating spirit which boils over in anger, that one feels the mark of an unsanctified soul. We may be hurt, but we also commit and trust it to God.

9. Joy is not always overflowing in the hearts of the sanctified. Heavy trials will produce a heaviness of spirit (1 Peter 1:6-9).

These trials are profitable, really indispensable.

Sanctification restores the soul. It purifies the affections and motives of the life, it lifts all of life up to a plane of holiness and love, but it leaves us men and women. Do not expect impossibilities of it, but expect it to cleanse out sin and carnal wicked elements.

God's plan for the earth is for salvation to extend to all men until this world shall be ruled by divine principles and love instead of lust and selfishness.

44   ADVENTURES IN THE LAND OF CANAAN

Give yourself wholly to God, then, dear soul; fully yield all up to the divine will and care not how you feel. Let God care for your feelings as well as for everything else. He will "keep him in perfect peace whose mind is stayed on" Him. Glorious peace, precious rest, delightful confidence!

A certain woman lived a precarious existence, but she was so happy in her life with Jesus that she was the marvel of her town.

You have given all to God, let Him keep all of you and for you.

CHAPTER ELEVEN
THE ROUTING OF GIANT DOUBT

Doubts! doubts! doubts! Just a company of them around me all the time worse than Job's miserable comforters. What can I do with them? I should like to dismiss them, but it seems I can not. They make me much trouble, but it seems I can not get them to leave me. Especially are the doubts concerning my entire consecration aggravating, and those, too, concerning my entire cleansing. I fear to come out boldly and declare that I believe that Christ fully saves me now. I believe He can and will, but the words die on my lips when I attempt to bring it down to the present moment. Yet I know these doubts are dishonoring to God, who has made such great and glorious promises. Can you give me some instructions on what to do with doubts? How did you overcome yours? Please help me, in Christ's name.

* * * * *

Pilgrim Sincere lives in what I hear is one of the best parts of Canaan. He had a great encounter with old Giant Doubt; so let us pay him a visit. We have met the old Giant already, and we have no hesitation in saying that if there is a worse giant than he in Canaan, we are not eager to meet him. Pilgrim Sincere may tell us something about him that it will be of profit to us to know.

Here! We are at Sincere's place already. There is no question of his victory over Giant Doubt. Such a shield of faith as his is I never saw before!

"Pilgrim Sincere, we have been talking with pilgrims and residents of Canaan, and now we have come to see you. Will you tell us something that will enable us to gain a freehold in Canaan? We have met many poor pilgrims who say they have never yet gained a clear title to a home here. They have been driven here and there by this or that old giant. We are eager not to be defeated in this great adventure in Canaan."

"If you will give all honor to Immanuel and none to me, I will relate my experiences—a few at least. There are many giants in Canaan, very many of them. There is Giant Lust, who has slain thousands. Poor souls! Giant Puff-up, who causes pilgrims to act as foolish as did the toad that saw an elephant and burst itself trying to be as large; Giant Lethargy, who operates an opiate factory in a hollow that runs directly down into Egypt; Giant Covetousness, who decoys pilgrims to the silver-mine run by Balaam and Demas; Giant Pride, an evil giant who has troubled pilgrims for time out of mind; Giant Liar, who uses an abundance of camouflage; and others [Galatians 5:19-21]."

46 ADVENTURES IN THE LAND OF CANAAN

"My, you almost scare us naming them! Can it be we must fight all of them? Is not this that rest-land!"

"My dear pilgrims, this is Beulah-land, and Sabbath-land. Here is the true rest. But remember, Canaan has its giants, more so than the wilderness; the true rest is found in overcoming them. Do not be frightened. Look at the armor with which you are equipped."

"Sincere, the armor is all right, but it is ourselves that we are doubtful of. Can we use the sword and the shield as they should be used?"

"Indeed you can, pilgrims, no doubt of it. Why, when I got into Canaan I was so weak I nearly lost my life fighting."

"Tell us about it."

"About twenty-five years ago I entered Canaan. It was a great day for me! At last the long journey through the wilderness was over, the deep, wide waters of Jordan passed! Canaan was my own! I praised Immanuel and began to possess the land [Joshua 1:2, 3].

"Not long after that I met a lean, white-whiskered man named Legality. He said he was my friend. He looked venerable and sincere, even if he did appear rather stern and immovable! 'Now friend Sincere,' he said, 'I have something here that will help you walk safely and straight,' and with that he slipped a peculiar jacket over my head and buckled it up pretty tight around my waist [Galatians 5:1].

"'There,' he said, 'that jacket just fits you. You are in Canaan now, and must walk, oh, so straight and carefully! Why, if you make even ever so little a mistake, you will be punished, I fear, dreadfully. But that jacket will help you and keep you from doing anything far out of the way.' And with that he left me.

"Well, I wanted anything that would help me, so I kept the jacket on. It bothered me considerably. It was made of stiff, iron stays, woven in with rough haircloth, both of which were made, so Mr. Legality said, by one Mr. Over-Conscientious Scruple who lives in the town of Sensitive.

"Every move I made was retarded by that jacket. By and by sore places appeared where the end of the stays engaged my flesh. I met Mr. Legality once and told him how bad the jacket was treating me, but he said the cure was to buckle it on tighter. Oh, my, how it did hurt! But he said it would be dangerous to take it off. So I continued to suffer. I could not act freely in any matter.

"Just about this time old Giant Doubt met me. He carried a book and a big pencil. 'Sit down here while I give you an examination; that is my business,' he said. 'My lord has commissioned me to do this work.' Something inside me told me that here was an enemy; but he spoke with such a show of authority that I passively sat down. And he began.

"'How do you feel?'

"'I do not feel very good, just now.' I said.

THE ROUTING OF GIANT DOUBT   **47**

"'I thought so. No doubt there is something wrong with you. Have you gained an established home in Canaan yet?'

"'No, I haven't,' I replied.

"'Well, you never will; at least there are serious doubts about it. It is my business to make sure that pilgrims possess the land. Did you put up your memorial stone!'

"'Yes, I carried a stone out of the middle of Jordan and set it up. I suppose it is there yet.'

"'That stone was no good, a little rough rock it was. Why didn't you select a nice large stone such as Pilgrim Joyful carried out?'

"'I did the best I could; that was the only stone I saw in passing through. I noticed it was not like Pilgrim Joyful's, and not like Pilgrim Honest's, either.'

"'No good, no good! Too small! I doubt if it is really stone at all. Did you leave all the wilderness luggage on yonder side Jordan?'

"'I intended to. I dropped the whole bundle as I stepped into the Jordan.'

"'I doubt it. I believe you have considerable wilderness trappings in your possession. More than that, I doubt whether you left all your load when you crossed the Red Sea. Did you?'

"'I thought I did,' I replied.

"'I doubt it. How do you feel now?' said old Giant Doubt.

"'I feel bad, worse than before the examination began.' I replied.

"'I see you do. Something is wrong with you. You have passed a poor examination. It is my business to carry you out of Canaan as unworthy to be in this good land. Come on,' and with that he arose and advanced toward me with both hands extended. I trembled violently, but seemed powerless to resist. He picked me up and started off with me. Just then I spotted a sturdy post with a sign-board nailed to the top. I eagerly sought to read the legend. 'Beware!' it began. 'At this place a certain old giant, named Doubt, has a habit of stopping pilgrims and taking them through a pretended examination. He claims to hold a commission from his lord to do this work. His commission is true; but his lord is Beelzebub. After the examination, he usually carries off the pilgrim who allows him to question him. Many have fallen to his devices. He is a cruel, old giant, and he carries his victims to' — and here I could read no more.

"We soon left the main road and entered a dark valley called Vale of Destruction.

"'Let me go,' I shouted.

"'I will not, you are not fit to be in Canaan,' he replied.

"I struggled and shouted for help with all my might. He held me close, however, and the vale grew darker and darker.

"'O Immanuel, do send me help! Oh, deliver me from this cruel giant!' I cried.

48   ADVENTURES IN THE LAND OF CANAAN

Just then there appeared ahead a stream of light, which came in from one side of the valley. When we reached the light, I saw a beautiful mansion built high up on the sides of a valley that broadened out in a beautiful vale named Hope. Some people were singing on the lawn of the mansion. Either they caught a glimpse of the old giant carrying me, or my loud shouts for help reached them. At any rate, I saw two of them start toward us [Galatians 6:2].

"Old Giant Doubt attempted to run faster, as he also caught sight of them; but a periodic rheumatism attacked him, and he made little progress. The two pilgrims, who I found were Valiant and Faithful, rushed to my rescue.

"'You wicked old Giant Doubt,' they shouted, 'let go of Pilgrim Sincere.'

And they attacked him with their swords.

"'Sincere,' they cried, 'take your sword and use it!'

"By this time my arm was free enough to grasp the sword, and I gave the giant a close thrust. At this he dropped me and ran as fast as he could.

"'Poor pilgrim,' said Valiant. 'How fortunate for you that you shouted! We heard the call. Praise and honor to Immanuel.' And Valiant reverently lifted his hands and eyes heavenward.

"'Where did the old, evil giant overcome you?' asked Faithful.

"'Back at a place where there is a sign warning pilgrims against Giant Doubt. But I did not see the sign till he started off with me.'

"'I wonder if we can not mark that spot more plainly, so that no pilgrim will ever allow Giant Doubt to hold his false examination there?' asked Valiant.

"'No,' said Faithful. 'It has been tried over and over. No sign except the one that is there ever remains even if it is put up.'

"'What kind of garment is that you are wearing around your waist?' asked Faithful.

"'This is a jacket that Mr. Legality gave me to wear.' I answered.

"'The crafty villain,' exclaimed Faithful. 'Put it away from you!'

"But I was afraid to do this, and told them so. They related how that same jacket had caused them much trouble. They further said that no one could unbuckle it but me, as there was a secret lock on each jacket that no one but the wearer could work.

"After this I got back to the main highway again. But the first thing I knew was that old Giant Doubt was with me again [Matthew 14:28-31]. And he began to talk to me just as if he had never said anything to me before. I wondered what I should do if he attempted to carry me away. And then I remembered what I read on a monument just after crossing the Jordan: 'Every pilgrim must overcome the giants for himself.' But just how to do this I did not know. So I had another encounter with him.

"'Do you still think you are a pilgrim in Canaan?' he said. 'More than likely

THE ROUTING OF GIANT DOUBT 49

you will never find rest. I doubt it very much. See how bad you feel. And you are always saying or doing something that hurts you. Pilgrims should live better than you do.' And with that he grabbed me in his big, burly arms and nearly squeezed the life out of me. I couldn't fight at all. The jacket held me so rigid that I could not even use the sword or hold up the shield. In fact, Mr. Legality told me his straight-jacket was a better protection than any sword or shield; and I had gradually grown into dependency on it.

"Next day Giant Doubt assailed me again. This time he unmercifully beat me with his wormwood club. And after cuffing me about until I was nearly dead, he again left me. Then he came every day. It is peculiar how long he kept my company. Or, rather, it is strange how long I allowed him to be with me. And every day I found myself weaker; and when the old giant threatened to throw me into the sea of the dead, I had very little resistance in me—just enough to keep him from his purpose.

"I found that every time I used the sword ever so little it scared the old giant; and when he shot hot darts, I found that the shield would stop them if I held it up. But that old jacket was very much in my way.

"At last I said to myself, 'I believe this jacket is a nuisance. Off with it!' and I pulled it off and threw it as far as I could down into the crevasse of Worn Out Laws [James 1:25].

"After this, I met Giant Doubt again. But my wounds had become well, and I determined to fight for my life and my liberty. I told the giant that, Immanuel helping me, I should not let him travel with me another step of the way.

"'Oh, yes I will!' he said. 'You can not travel without me. I'm your friend.'

"'You are no friend,' I cried, 'but an enemy. You have made my journey miserable. You have driven away my peace; you have killed my joy; you have beaten me, deceived me, and threatened me with death, and have indeed nearly killed me. Go! Get behind me! you enemy of my soul' [Matthew 4:1-11].

"And at this I smote him with the sword of truth. He ran away and got out his arrows to shoot at me as before; but I simply held up the shield, and not one hurt me [Romans 16:20]. Then I ran after him with all my might and chased him away—and I haven't had a real encounter with him since."

* * * * *

The cure for doubts is faith; not prayer, nor fasting, nor working— just faith. Faith is believing God, believing just what God says. God has said many things and made many promises. Faith expects God to fulfill His word. Trust is faith holding on and waiting.

We are sanctified by faith; we enter into complete soul-rest by faith. There is no other way. We must come to God and simply ask Him to work His complete redemption in our hearts and fill us with the Spirit. After we give ourselves wholly to Him, after we lay all on the altar, there is nothing more that we can do except trust and obey. It is God's part to complete in us the work for salvation; our business is to trust Him to do it. We trust carpenters and builders to build our houses,

50 ADVENTURES IN THE LAND OF CANAAN

we trust bankers with our money, we trust men every day and hour of our lives; shall we not trust God?

In all battles with doubt, go back to basic facts. Allow no confusion of mind, no agitation of spirit; calm every fear and find out just where and how you are. First, ask yourself if you are all the Lord's. Do you now lay on His altar your all? Do you now choose His will? Do you intend to serve Him? Do you answer, "Yes"? Put that down then as a settled fact. Never allow yourself to doubt a point that has been settled. Let it stay settled. Next ask yourself if you believe God is true to His word, if you believe He will do what He promised. If you say, "Yes," let that point be settled also. Stand by it. If you have met the conditions upon which God promised to cleanse and fill you, you must believe that God does these things for you.

Doubts have a way of coming in early in the morning. They are like bad neighbors, they come when they are not wanted. Doubts may arise because you do not "feel" as you should like to, or because you have made mistakes; or simply because you have been sorely tempted. You must learn that feeling is no true gage of your spiritual experience.

An encounter with doubts may be something like this: You awake in the morning and are possessed of a feeling that is utterly non-religious. You do not feel one whit as though you are fully saved and trusting, but just the opposite. Not having learned to pay no attention to this, but instead to jump up and praise and thank God for all His goodness, you begin to question, "Am I really and truly consecrated? Where are all my joyful feelings? Why do I feel this way? Surely something is wrong."

The longer you think, the more doubtful you become, and at last discouragement takes charge of your whole soul.

There is no harm, but good, in examining ourselves; it is all right to put hard and searching questions to our hearts as to our standing with God. But when doubts lead to such an examination, the result is usually disastrous.

Doubting gets to be a bad habit; one very hard to break. It is a sort of self-depreciating, self-deprecating, self-condemning habit. Doubting becomes easy and natural after the habit is formed. A chronic state of discouragement follows. You are as miserable as you can be. And yet the idea of abruptly cutting off the whole bad thing fills you with dismay. You are afraid to do it. A sort of up-and-down life seems preferable to a bold, upstanding victorious life. A sort of weakness or spiritual cowardice follows, too; and one habitually doubting prefers to be a pygmy, a dwarf, for Christ, rather than a real man, a warrior in Him.

Doubt has a dreadful reaction on the soul and mind. Its influence is deadening and damning. It shrivels and dries up the joy and spontaneity of service. It makes one feel inferior and weak. Instead of causing one to fight, doubts lead one to give up the fight; instead of prompting resistance, doubts make one lie down and get wounded and bruised. Doubts make us failures. They blight, mar, and drag down. They are the devil's own poison to kill off God's people.

There is only one thing to do to overcome doubts: have faith in God. Kill the

THE ROUTING OF GIANT DOUBT 51

doubts, or they will kill you. "This is the victory that overcometh the world, even our faith" (1 John 5:4).

CHAPTER TWELVE
THE WINE OF PRAYER

I am troubled with listlessness in prayer. When I kneel to pray, my mind wanders here and there out over the world—to my business, or probably to some trifling thing that amounts to nothing. I feel chagrined and disappointed. Jesus is so loyal to me, so worthy of praise and prayer, that to feel thus in prayer is mortifying. I have confessed it, but have not obtained a satisfactory deliverance, nor a solution of the matter. Can you give me any help? It will be much appreciated if you can teach me how to feel unction in prayer, and how to pray the fervent prayer of the righteous. Oh, do help me! My heart longs, yea yearns, for that nearness to God in prayer that will draw out my soul in mighty petitions for others, especially for the suffering and the lost.

* * * * *

We heard of the fruits of Canaan long before we arrived. There were grapes of Eschol, pomegranates, milk and honey, and the old corn and wine of the land. Back in the Wilderness we were told of fruits so wonderful that they made the pilgrims strong and valiant for Immanuel, and of course we were eager to pluck them for ourselves. But we found that every one must grow or gather his own fruit, and also that the finest food is obtained from the most unlikely places, on hard, stony soil, and in rather inaccessible spots.

For instance, the honey. Hardly any of this delightful food was obtainable except in the crags of Hard Trials Mountains. And the Wine of Prayer was pressed from grapes that grew best in the Valley of Sore Temptation.

Do you suppose Caleb could tell us how to obtain these fruits? We are specially interested in the Wine of Prayer, suppose we go and see Caleb today. He received us so graciously on our former visit, he probably would be glad to see us again. Let us go!

Yes, he is at home today. See, there he is now. Oh, he is on his knees! Dear old saint of Canaan! And what is that he is doing? Oh, see, he seems to be drawing something from a cask in the shades of his beautiful garden! Yes, indeed, that must be Wine of Prayer he is drawing! What a blessed favor to call upon Him on such an occasion. He does not see us. Let us wait here, apart from his sanctuary.

Caleb seems lost in earnest communion with Immanuel. Note the heavenly smile that lights up his weather-beaten old face! He seems animated by the draughts he takes from his wine-cask. When his devotions and communions are

THE WINE OF PRAYER

over, we shall greet him. See, he rises! What a glory emanates from his face! It causes me to feel eager to slake my thirst at the same holy place! My life seems so earthly, so lacking in heavenliness and saintliness!

"Pilgrim Caleb, do tell us what you were drinking and how we may obtain some of the same wine."

"Most gladly. First, I must tell you a secret. The grapes from which the best Wine of Prayer is made come from the Valley of Sore Temptation. That is not a pleasant place, by any means. Several bad giants rendezvous there. Old Giants Lust, Pride, Persecution, Worldliness, Covetousness, and others make it a sort of headquarters. They never bother the grape-vines; it is only the pilgrims that they annoy. The soil is rocky and hard to subdue and cultivate. I wanted the very best fruits the land had; so I, too, was obliged to take a plot of ground in the Valley of Sore Temptation and make a beginning.

"No sooner had I marked off my little plot than the giants haunted me. They buffeted me about rather rudely. Old Giant Pride tried to make me think I was one of the greatest men who ever came into Canaan. Old Giant Covetousness told me all about a silver-mine which Balaam opened and Demas worked in. I could easily get rich, he said, if I would abandon the cultivation of grapes and follow him to the mine. He certainly told a plausible story, and tried hard to influence me to go. Giant Lust pointed out ways and means to capture silly souls, and tried hard to attract my attention toward a valley that leads down into Egypt; I had had enough of Egypt, and resisted him with all my might. But no matter how hard I resisted or rebuked these giants, they stayed in that valley. No one, it seems, can rout them completely from it. Their presence there goes with the cultivation of grapes.

"Well, I grew a small crop the first season. Then I made a wine-press out of pieces of faith, patience, and obedience, and placed a heavy weight on top made of perseverance. I got a little wine, and, oh, it was delicious and refreshing! Since then I have learned more about raising the fruit and making wine. I can get more wine out of the grapes, too, than formerly, by getting a heavier weight and using larger pieces of material in the press.

"Nothing is so refreshing as the Wine of Prayer. The whole soul is caught up, invigorated, revitalized, inspired. It gives mighty strength. Giants tremble and quake and run for their lives when they see a pilgrim fresh from his wine-cask move upon them. Blessed be Immanuel! Glory, praise, and honor, hallelujah to His high name, forever and ever! Oh, He provides such power and unction and sweetness! Never rest, pilgrims, till you get your vineyard started. And may Immanuel bless you!"

Thanks to Caleb for his words!

Listlessness in prayer is the result of a lack of interest; no one is listless about things he is vitally interested in. The thing to do is, not work against listlessness, for listlessness is only a symptom, but work up a real interest in the object of prayer. Find something to pray for, and pray for it with all your might.

Mind-wandering during secret prayer can also be attributed to lack of interest

54　ADVENTURES IN THE LAND OF CANAAN

in the right thing. If your mind wanders, it is no sin, but a sign that you have nothing very pressing to pray for. If you were wanting something which you needed very much—if you were sorely and severely tempted, or were sick and suffering, or if you were persecuted and needed help—you would pray earnestly enough. Or, if you had in mind a friend or relative who was in need of help, then you could pray earnestly.

The cure for listlessness and mind-wandering, therefore, is in feeling and knowing the need, either of ourselves or of others, for which we engage in prayer. There is too much need for any listlessness in prayer. To be sure, no one can always feel the same degree of fervor and unction in prayer; but there may always be enough to make prayer a really refreshing season to the soul.

Prayer is more than asking; it is praise, thanksgiving, communion. We are exhorted "to be careful for nothing; but in everything by prayer and supplication with thanksgiving let your requests be made known unto God" (Philippians 4:6). Prayer, then, is partly thanksgiving.

Begin with thanksgiving. If the Lord has done anything for you, thank Him for it. Count your blessings as you kneel. Remember the pit of sin you were taken out of; consider how often you have been helped and protected. Exercising the soul in this way produces the most favorable state of mind for further prayer, for making requests.

Give God a chance to talk to you while you are in prayer. Ask for a conversation. Be still and listen for God's voice; expect Him to speak.

In making requests, be willing for God to have His way. Ask, and you shall receive; but not always as soon as you ask.

Importunity in prayer is needed as well as perseverance and patience.

It is a blessed thing, this life of trust, the life of prayer. In daily communion with Christ we may travel life's road and enjoy a fellowship too rich, too deep, too holy to describe adequately. Enter in and see and taste for yourself.

CHAPTER THIRTEEN
PILGRIMS OF THE VICTORIOUS LIFE

Please tell me, will you, if a really victorious life is possible to me; I mean a day-by-day, year-in-and-year-out experience? I have so much of struggle and battle in my life that a life of constant victory seems a vague, faraway dream. It seems to me that the only ones capable of obtaining and retaining this blissful state are those living very sheltered lives and with few obstacles in their way. These may live victoriously; but as for me, with my toils and troubles of various kinds, how can it be possible? I have met many victorious Christians. Of course I do not know how it is with them; but I believe their sweet temper pointed plainly to the fact that their lives had fallen in very pleasant places. Can you give me any clue to this matter? If a victorious life is possible for me, I want it. Will you help me? Thank you!

* * * * *

Well, upon my word! There goes Pilgrim Serene, who lives in Poverty Vale, close by Caleb's fair Hebron home! Shall we engage her in conversation? They say she is one of the sweetest-tempered pilgrims in Canaan, and yet we are told that her home is in one of the poorest spots in the land. And who is that walking by her side! She seems to be very happy. Oh, yes, that is Pilgrim Joyful! And where does she live? They say she lives in Trouble Hollow, close by Offense Mountain. My, those names sound ominous, don't they! Do let us engage them in conversation; for it seems sweeter faced pilgrims we never have seen.

"May we walk with you in the way? And may we inquire about your home in Canaan, and why it is you seem so happy and calm? We are only a few days over the Jordan, and are trying to learn all we can of the land. Where did you get those beautiful flowers in your hands? Tell us your experiences! Please do!"

"You are welcome to our company, gladly. I am Pilgrim Serene; my companion is Pilgrim Joyful. These flowers came from the garden of Patient Endurance, which is situated on Mount Calm. The flowers are free to all pilgrims; but the road to the garden is a very rough road, and thorn-bushes fringe it for a considerable distance. Some pilgrims once organized a band to clear out the thorns; but the bushes have such a tough bark that no knife was able to cut through them. So they stand there still. Another band gathered out all the stones; but new stones fall from the cliffs above all the time, and some of the new stones are worse to cut the feet of pilgrims than the old ones were. So it is thought best to let the path alone. Just smell how sweet these are!"

"Where do you live, Pilgrim Serene?"

56   ADVENTURES IN THE LAND OF CANAAN

"I live in Poverty Vale. The floor of the valley is very hard and poor. But Immanuel walks and talks with me. Every day He comes and helps me; every day He lifts burdens off my back. Showers of blessing fall every day or two."

"You never have any trouble do you, Pilgrim Serene? I am sure you do not; for you look so free from care and worry."

"My dear pilgrim, I have a struggle all the time. I never know what it is to be free from pain or poverty. If it were not for Honey Rock, I certainly should have famished long ago."

"Where is Honey Rock?"

"Oh, it borders the Vale, high up in the mountains. Only a faint path leads to it; for it seems only a few pilgrims know where it is. And besides, it is the roughest path I ever tried to follow. But once one is at the Rock, all one has to do to feast on the nectar is to smite the Rock in the name of Immanuel, and forthwith there comes out the most delicious honey in all the world."

"Oh, we wish to eat of it! But, there is that rough foot-path. I don't know whether we can walk it or not!"

"Have you been to Honey Rock too, Pilgrim Joyful?"

"Yes, pilgrims, I have. I was there yesterday."

"Is it that which caused the scratches and blood stains on your feet and hands and which tore your garments?"

"Yes, pilgrims. As to my home, it is in Trouble Hollow. Offense Mountain rises high on two sides of it. Not many pilgrims like my home; but Immanuel gave it to me, and any home in Canaan is preferable to the best spot in the Wilderness, better than the grandest mansion in Egypt. It is true my home is in a dark valley, and old Offense Mountain has continual landslides that I have to help clear away; but, glory and praises to Immanuel! a bare existence in Canaan surpasses anything I ever enjoyed before. Hallelujah! Angels in bands visit me often. Heaven seems in sight!"

"Thank you Serene and Joyful. We shall be glad to meet you again."

These two pilgrims whose lives are spent in Canaan's most troubled spots have a holy serenity that shames us when we think of how we complain at a few hard things that we have met. Thank God for such pilgrims!

Here is a true story. Mrs. B— — is a cripple woman who walks with a crutch. Years ago she was converted and later was wholly sanctified. Her husband was a wicked man who gave her a great deal of trouble and at last died and left her with several children. They were miserably poor. She took her family overland for a hundred miles to another place, walking and carrying their effects as best they could. She is still poor, though her children have now become self-supporting. No one could think of anything harder to go through with than this woman had. Her physical handicap prevented her doing many things she could otherwise have done, she was compelled to work at the hardest jobs, and had to see her children grow up without schooling. All was hard; just plain, hard living. If the family had

PILGRIMS OF THE VICTORIOUS LIFE   57

enough to eat, it was a thing to be thankful for. And yet, in those years this woman has always been cheerful, and gives a brilliant testimony to the grace of God to keep her sweet and joyful.

Another case is that of "Brother H," we shall call him. Brother H was afflicted with tuberculosis. He was called to the ministry, was a splendid singer, mightily gifted in prayer, and was used of God in working several remarkable miracles of healing. His family was numerous, much more so than his afflicted condition made possible for him to support. He lived in a small three-room house, with eight or nine children and an overburdened wife. He could do no work. His neighbors frowned on him and persecuted him mildly for not working. His home was the very picture of poverty; nothing could be worse in that line, scarcely. Yet he was a man of the highest Christian integrity and faith, and was one of the happiest Christians one could meet. And his happiness was not that of the careless man, not the happiness of a callous, uneducated person; for he felt keenly the poverty to which he was subjected and was always embarrassed at his state and the condition of his home. He had that fine intuition and grace of a gentleman of the highest order; and yet he was happy in the Lord. His happiness was the genuine joy of full salvation in his heart, born of a faith that believed all things were working together for his good.

Entire sanctification is not something that takes troubles out of the life, neither does it change one's outward circumstances; but it does lift the soul above all earthly troubles and let it soar in God's free air of victory.

To the fully consecrated soul there are no "second causes"; that is, no one is between him and God who can harm him or affect him in any way apart from God's will. It may be that others will mistreat us grievously, and their acts be wrong and utterly opposed to God's will; but those acts have had to pass God's will in getting to us. By this they become the will of God to us. For instance, some one may persecute us. The spirit of persecution is wicked and God has nothing to do with it; but before that persecution reaches us it must pass God's will; so the persecution becomes God's will to us, and we bear it for His sake. God may put some bad medicine in human bottles and cause us to drink of them for our good.

This victorious life is a life on wings. We are to mount up with wings as eagles. The wings are faith and consecration. When troubles come, we flap our wings and fly over them. Since we are God's, it is His place to bring us out and help us over, hence the fully consecrated soul trusts, and lets God work matters out. Of course, this does not mean that we shall not help ourselves. In fact, little trust can be exercised until we have done all we can do to help ourselves; but if we can not avail or prevail, we carry it to the Lord and leave it with Him to work out.

David speaks of the Lord's hiding him in His secret place, in His pavilion, under His wings. Jesus has said that not a hair of our head shall fall without our Father's notice. Peter says we are to cast all our care upon God, for God careth for us. And Paul exhorts us to be careful for nothing, but with prayer and thanksgiving let our requests be known to God.

The greatest of all comforts is this, "We know that all things work together

58   **ADVENTURES IN THE LAND OF CANAAN**

for good to them that love God" (Romans 8:28). "All things" means *all things*. The Christian who gives up all is certain of God's continual care and protection. He can not expect to escape trouble or trial or temptation; but he is kept in these things. "Thou wilt keep him in perfect peace whose mind is stayed on thee." "Great peace have they which love thy law: and nothing shall offend them." That is, nothing shall cause them to fall. They may be hurt, and be wounded by the inconsiderate or deliberate acts or words of others; but they will sail on in peace in God.

The will of God surrounds us like a wall, and nothing can penetrate that wall and touch our consecrated souls unless God so wills, or permits.

Of all lives, the victorious life is the richest and best. There is joy in serving, giving, sacrificing. If we are persecuted for Christ's sake, there is great joy. Life's problems are met with faith. A colored woman who had to wash for a living was very happy all the time. Rich women would marvel at her peace of mind, and one time one of them chided her for her optimism, which to the rich woman seemed based on nothing. "Why, suppose you should get sick, or suppose something should happen," said her rich friend. "Oh, I never supposes," said the poor woman. "That is what is the matter with you, you supposes and supposes and imagines all lands of ill coming on you. The Lord is my shepherd, and I shall not want. So I never supposes, I know everything will come out all right." She just flapped her wings, so to speak, and flew over her troubles.

The victorious life is free from worry, fretting, overanxious solicitude, burdensome care. It is free from malice, ill will, retaliation. It is free from bad temper, sees the bright side of things, and wears its clouds inside out. The sanctified life is a life of faith, and it is a life of obedience. To trust has to it become a habit, to obey a second nature. The victorious life looks not behind, but ahead; it ignores past failures and goes forward in faith.

And this victorious life is for all. Instead of being for favored folk, it is for the weak, the burdened, the poor, the sick, the troubled, the persecuted. Enter in by consecration and faith. Yield all just now. Lay all on God's altar. Be His alone. Then by faith enter into this life which will be yours every day as you live by faith and trust and obey.

Lector House believes that a society develops through a two-fold approach of continuous learning and adaptation, which is derived from the study of classic literary works spread across the historic timeline of literature records. Therefore, we aim at reviving, repairing and redeveloping all those inaccessible or damaged but historically as well as culturally important literature across subjects so that the future generations may have an opportunity to study and learn from past works to embark upon a journey of creating a better future.

This book is a result of an effort made by Lector House towards making a contribution to the preservation and repair of original ancient works which might hold historical significance to the approach of continuous learning across subjects.

HAPPY READING & LEARNING!

LECTOR HOUSE LLP
E-MAIL: lectorpublishing@gmail.com